HYPNOSIS

HEALING AND

THE CHRISTIAN

HYPNOSIS

HEALING AND

THE CHRISTIAN

John H. Court

Foreword by John Hall

Wipf and Stock Publishers
EUGENE, OREGON

Wipf and Stock Publishers
199 West 8th Avenue, Suite 3
Eugene, Oregon 97401

Hypnosis Healing and the Christian
By Court, John H.

ISBN: 1-57910-982-9
Publication date: June, 2002
Previously published by Paternoster Press, 1997.

Contents

Foreword

Hypnosis is, to many people, a strange and threatening phenomenon. Perhaps the two most common stereotypes of a hypnotist are, on the one hand, a sinister Svengali-like figure out to exploit the vulnerable and, on the other hand, an experienced performer out to amuse by eliciting strange and embarrassing behaviour. For Christians there is another dimension – is hypnosis in some way evil, and should Christians ever permit themselves to be hypnotized?

John Court's book offers a very thorough exploration of the aspects of hypnosis that are of interest and concern to Christians. He writes from his own extensive experience of the clinical use of hypnosis as well as his academic research into hypnosis. As a clinical psychologist he has worked in three continents – having started his career in Britain, he continued it at universities in Australia, then moved as Professor to Fuller Seminary in Pasadena, and has now returned to Australia. Hypnosis is not the only field in which Dr Court has sought to integrate his faith and his profession; he is very involved in the training of pastoral counsellors, and has played a key role in presenting a Christian perspective on pornography and its psychological effects.

One of the most valuable aspects of this book is the way in which hypnosis is demythologized and presented as one among a number of different altered states of consciousness. Hypnosis is presented as a phenomenon that can be understood in terms of contemporary psychology; and hypnotizability is shown to be an attribute of *ourselves*, and not of the hypnotist.

Hypnosis is further presented as a skilled therapeutic procedure which, when practised by those already qualified in a health care profession, may have positive benefits comparable to other well-established methods, without the side-effects which may arise from medication. Specific examples referred to include the use of hypnotic techniques to treat emotional problems within a psychotherapeutic relationship, and to induce anaesthesia in dental practice.

It is important that Christians understand hypnosis, not only for its own significance, but because of the real or supposed links between hypnosis and other phenomena, including some charismatic manifestations and the extreme suggestibility which is sometimes apparent in small religious groups. Understanding hypnosis helps us to understand our own responses, and those of others, when confronted with powerful and persuasive suggestions, secular or spiritual. Conversely, it safeguards us from unwittingly using techniques of communication or persuasion that discourage others from using their full, God-given understanding and free will.

John Court head-on confronts those writers who suggest that hypnosis is self-evidently demonic. He carefully analyses the biblical texts most frequently appealed to, quotes abundantly from pastoral and clinical case studies in order to examine their pastoral implications, and considers, for example, the complex issue of a possible relationship between hypnosis and New Age practices.

This is a thoughtful and thorough book, written by an international expert who is fully aware of the range of cultural attitudes towards, and contexts surrounding, the use of hypnosis. His practical clinical acuity and his wisdom in exploring the inter-relationships between hypnosis, spirituality, and healing shine through the book, making it invaluable to Christian ministers, counsellors and therapists, and to individual Christians wondering whether they themselves may find hypnosis helpful.

Introduction

The subject of hypnosis is not well understood beyond the domain of those who use it. The word itself is capable of conjuring up many responses: from those who have seen stage demonstrations, to those who have vague ideas that it is dangerous, and including those who have experienced the hypnotic state.

Within the church there are more negative reactions to it than positive ones, such that anyone claiming to be involved in hypnosis is likely to be viewed askance. While there are certainly some who speak favourably of its use and advocate hypnosis as a valuable resource, there are others who vehemently disapprove of it, often linking it with occultic practices, claiming demonic dangers and warning that Scripture condemns its use.

If indeed such concerns are soundly based, then Christians should be adequately warned and directed to avoid any involvement in hypnosis, both in using it with others and as a subject. If, on the other hand, such concerns are baseless, and the claims made for its healing effectiveness are justified, then it would be a serious matter to deny access to something able to bring health and healing. False warnings would be comparable to forbidding people to accept surgery and blood transfusions on religious grounds.

A third possibility, and the one to be advanced here, is that hypnosis could have a wide range of benefits when properly understood. At the same time, some cautions are in order for anyone who might wish to explore it and especially for Christians, for whom questions of influence and control over behaviour and thought represent significant issues of personal faith and theology.

Hypnosis is one of many concepts which represent a clash of cultures. It is historically embedded in religious practices, and has a known history spanning thousands of years. Yet the word itself is of recent origin, and derives from the world of scientific enquiry. 'Hypnotism' was the term introduced by a British physician, James Braid, in 1843, later modified to 'hypnosis'. It has been developed for secular therapeutic purposes, and is studied extensively as a scientific phenomenon, even though it involves subjectivity of experience and often relates more closely to the world of mysticism.

There is a close parallel here with the recent history of the term 'psychology'. While theories of psychology are commonly traced back to the great days of Greece and linked with names like Hippocrates, the father of medicine, the word itself is of recent origin, and the scientific study of psychology is commonly considered to have emerged in the late nineteenth century. Through the centuries, psychological phenomena and religious practices have commonly blended together, to the extent that they might be considered inextricably intertwined, yet in recent years psychology has been roundly attacked by some as anti-Christian and hostile to faith. The science versus religion debates of this century have revolved as much around psychology as they have around the evolutionary theory of Charles Darwin. Christians of various persuasions and traditions have fought vigorously on both sides of these debates, and scientists affirming a Christian faith have experienced the tension of two kinds of knowledge competing for pre-eminence.

Such debates are not trivial. They cause us to reflect on the sources of knowledge that we will respect. They highlight the tension existing when the revealed truth of the Bible encounters the discovered truth of scientific enquiry, resulting in a need either to favour one source over the other, or else to find common ground and ways of holding both kinds of truth as legitimate.

When a concept such as hypnosis is presented with both positive and negative connotations, we most easily move to a position of concluding either 'It is good' or 'It is bad'. When we have come to one of these conclusions, the most comfortable way of dealing with the other option is to dismiss any evidence which appears to challenge our view. If hypnosis is seen as bad, then we will discount any indications that it might be helpful, finding reasons which enable us to retain our belief intact, e.g. 'The healing was really due to prayer' or 'They would have recovered anyway.' If hypnosis is seen as good, then we will typically dismiss suggestions of danger or harm, finding reasons to attribute apparent harm to some other factor, e.g. 'The hypnotist was incompetent' or 'The person wasn't really hypnotized in the first place.'

It is more challenging to accept that something can have good and bad elements to it at the same time. It requires a higher level of discernment and critical thought to acknowledge that what is good can also be harmful, or that something which is usually harmful may also have positive uses. Nonetheless, this is a reality in many circumstances, of major and minor significance. A knife can be an efficient and helpful instrument for cutting, or a cause of real danger in the hands of a killer. Nuclear energy may provide electricity for the nation, yet also prove highly destructive. Religious belief may be the source of inspiration and the gateway to eternal life, or it may be pathologically obsessive leading to death and destruction.

From these examples not only may we conclude that hypnosis could have the powerful capacity for good and, at the same time, the potential for negative consequences. We may also see that those things which are particularly powerful have the potential for good and bad effects. Just as a powerful medicine can be very useful when administered therapeutically, yet deadly in other circumstances, so hypnosis can be very useful under the right circumstances, yet correspondingly provide a context for danger when abused.

Such preliminary comments set the stage for asking what hypnosis is, where it comes from, how it works, what it is useful for, and what the dangers are. In addition, the Christian should ask what is the relationship between hypnosis and religious experience, and the implications of using hypnosis to deal with issues that affect body, mind and spirit. Since religious experience extends well beyond Christian spirituality, we should consider the implications of something which has a place in religion generally, and whether it can be embraced within the Christian tradition without syncretism or heterodoxy.

In order for the reader to find where to start, and then pursue the topic, there are three major elements to the structure of this book. The opening sections, Chapters 2 to 3, deal with the concept of hypnosis from a theoretical point of view with commentary on what we know about it. There are many different opinions to consider, and I have related these to the myths about hypnosis that are widely believed.

The second theme, in Chapters 4 to 6, relates to the use of hypnosis in practical settings, showing through actual examples what may be achieved with this tool. The examples are deliberately chosen from experience with Christian people seeking help, in order to show how hypnotic techniques can be used without compromising faith, and further, to show how there can be a spiritual strengthening when Christian beliefs are incorporated in the therapeutic process.

Some readers may prefer to start with the third section, Chapters 7 and 8, which is more focused on the debate with those who argue that hypnosis is to be avoided by Christians. After discussing the reasons for such prohibitions, I provide responses to these arguments which place hypnosis not at some strange fringe of experience, but rather within its mainstream. This includes our world of spiritual experiences, and some of the phenomena of Christian spirituality are therefore also considered. While it is usual to consider such topics as inner healing, gifts of the Spirit, evangelism, and hypnosis as being distinct from one another, I prefer to emphasize their similarities, in the hope that Christian readers will be able to recognize not only the dangers but also the legitimacy of hypnotic phenomena.

One final point about the structure of what follows needs to be made. I have assumed that readers will not sit and read this book from cover to cover. As an educator, I assume that most readers will look initially for a section of particular interest, and then perhaps move to other sections. I also assume that information is absorbed best when it is provided in a context, and repeated from time to time. Hence, there are several themes here which I have addressed conceptually, then practically, and then again in the final critique. The repetition, dealing with issues such as dangers, false beliefs and anxieties, is deliberate in order to show how each issue relates to theory and practice. In order to make this process digestible for the average reader, and yet keep faith with those who wish to explore the current literature further, I have made use of footnotes by way of identifying related sources. These include material which I have published elsewhere, and which has been edited for this book. The case histories have all appeared as journal articles, and I acknowledge with appreciation permission to reprint material which has been granted by the editors of *Interchange, Journal of Christian Healing, Journal of Psychology and Christianity* and *Renewal Journal.*

Chapter 1

A Context for Understanding Hypnosis

If there were a simple answer to the question 'What is hypnosis?' there would be little to write about. It is because there are many ways of understanding hypnosis, because these are changing as evidence continues to come forward, and because there are so many preconceptions that the question deserves more than a simple formula.

For a long time there has been a mystique surrounding the practice of hypnosis, so that a collection of widespread, but incorrect, beliefs now exists. Some of these can be sorted out by first placing hypnosis in a broader context of knowledge about the way we perceive the world. Against this background, the most common misunderstandings will become clearer. This will naturally lead on to some reflection on Christian views of experiencing the world.

My starting point for this exploration is that hypnosis is one among many altered states of consciousness (ASCs). That is to say, we all shift our experience of the world in many ways during the course of a day, depending on the needs of a situation, and at these times we move from one state of consciousness to another. Sometimes we are very focused on a task, while at others we may be sleepy and inattentive. There are many variations and hypnosis is one part of the natural shifts that can occur.

This view of hypnosis as an ASC has been influential for a number of years. In adopting it as a basis for exploration here, it must be said that there are other ways of thinking about hypnosis. I cannot here explore the various schools of thought, but simply acknowledge that one particular approach is being adopted – probably the most useful one for relating hypnotic to spiritual experiences. The serious reader seeking a brief contemporary account of alternative viewpoints would be well-served by Kirsch and Lynn (1995).[1]

[1] Kirsch, I. & Lynn, S. J. (1995), 'The altered state of hypnosis', *American Psychologist, 50*, 10, 846–85.

Altered states of consciousness

This rather academic term, altered states of consciousness, provides a useful context for understanding that a number of shifts in our level of awareness occur as part of our normal human experience.[2] At the simplest level we know the difference between waking and sleeping. This very obvious ASC is measurable in many physiological ways, such as changes in breathing, body temperature, responsiveness to stimuli, and most clearly through the electrical record of brain activity (using the electro-encephalograph, or EEG). There are characteristic patterns of sleep rhythms which correspond to distinct phases of sleep. Another indisputable shift occurs when someone receives anaesthesia as an adjunct to surgery. Complete anaesthesia, in contrast to a locally-acting effect, results in a person losing consciousness for a period and has the desired effect of ensuring that pain perception is altered. A third obvious alteration occurs when someone drinks too much alcohol in a short time and becomes drunk. Under these circumstances a wide range of changes occur which are measurable (e.g. increased aggression, sleepiness, motor instability, slowed reaction times, impaired judgment). Subjectively, this ASC may be associated with a sense of euphoria, and later on, memory loss. A striking example of religious ASC is the fire-walker who may proceed to walk on heated coals without pain or burns. Whether as part of a religious ceremony, or as an entertainment for tourists, a shift of experience has occurred enabling the walker to do something most of us would consider to be impossible.

Such examples are taken to illustrate a much wider range of ASCs. They represent a range of phenomena which include the following:

(a) The natural rhythms of consciousness ranging from highly alert to completely unresponsive.
(b) Deliberate alterations to the state of consciousness to achieve a desired effect. A variant on this can be alteration to achieve escape from an undesired experience.
(c) Some ASCs arise without any external influences, while others

---

[2] Hilgard, E. R. (1977), *Divided consciousness: Multiple controls in human thought and action* (New York: Wiley). Although this term is the most widely used scientific term today, others argue persuasively for 'alternate states of consciousness' to affirm the continuity of experience. See esp. Zinberg, N. E. (1977), 'The study of consciousness states: Problems and progress', in N. E. Zinberg (ed), *Alternate states of consciousness*, (New York: Free Press); and Sheehan P. W. and McConkey, K. M. (1982), *Hypnosis and experience: The exploration of phenomena and process* (Hillsdale, NJ: Lawrence Erlbaum Associates).

depend on a substance to achieve the effect (most notably some form of drug).

(d) Some changes are transient, while others can be long-term or even permanent – the latter when brain biochemistry is affected. Some forms of psychotic illness and the long-term effects of alcoholism and drug addiction fall into this category.

(e) If there is a true distinction between secular and religious experience, then some ASCs are for secular purposes (e.g. anaesthetic) while others are for deliberate religious purposes (e.g. meditation).

Beyond the more obvious ASCs we then need to recognize that more subtle, hard-to-measure shifts are also a common part of human experience. These enable us to move towards an appreciation of the hypnotic experience, since features of these subtle ASCs often provide the gateway to a hypnotic state. A widely recognized example is sometimes called 'highway hypnosis'. The driver on a lengthy and familiar journey can travel a considerable distance with little awareness of what has happened, and then reflect 'I don't remember going past . . .' yet, clearly this has occurred. The 'tuning-out' of experience has some elements found also in true hypnosis.

As I write, with attention focused on ideas and how to express them, it becomes necessary to exclude extraneous noises in order to continue the task. I can become unaware of a doorbell ringing, of background conversation and passing traffic, selectively ignoring them as irrelevant or not needing attention. This ASC is a highly productive way of becoming absorbed in a task. A more intense form of this occurs on getting absorbed in a good story or watching a film, when reality and fantasy become blurred.

Many people are aware of an involuntary in-between world of consciousness when going to sleep or waking up. The dreams of true sleep can usually be recognized as such, but this halfway world of hypnogogic experiences is more confusing as we are unsure whether we *really* saw something, or only imagined it. Similarly, on returning from an anaesthetic, there can be a period of vague uncertainty with fluctuating consciousness such that the real and the imagined are not clearly distinguished.

The experience of something which is not present in reality is disturbing for most people, though deliberately pursued by others. The experience of hallucinations is an example of this, when visual or auditory (sometimes tactile) experience is reported, but nothing can be detected by another person. If I say 'There is a man standing in the doorway', but objectively this is not true, that is usually a worry and represents an ASC of some kind. It may be the symptom of a serious illness. Nonetheless, there are those who seek after and welcome such experiences, as when people have a deep longing to see a relative who is lost or has long since died. Seances seek to serve this longing to make contact. The alcoholic suffering delirium tremens (the 'DTs') will report experiences which cannot be verified by others. Clearly there is something happening in the brain which is abnormal, activating internal pathways, and perhaps firing off memories.

Among the less dramatic ASCs is the experience of prayer and meditation. Indeed the whole religious experience of private and corporate worship can induce ASCs which either occur involuntarily or, in many cases, are sought after. Should we dismiss as hallucinatory those who report hearing the voice of God speaking during times of spiritual retreat? Should we treat those who experience visions as sick? Should we follow those who burned Joan of Arc because of what she reported?

An alternative view would be that these experiences and the regular pursuits of the mystics have a legitimate purpose of accessing the spiritual world of reality through an ASC. As the regular impediments to deep concentration and sustained sensitivity are overcome, then a fuller awareness of the spiritual domain can be expected.

If this is not the case, then we should discontinue the collective and repetitive singing of such songs as 'Open our eyes, Lord, we want to see Jesus'. To those who do find such yearnings fulfilled in powerfully experienced imagery we may say that this has been achieved through an ASC.

Altered states, then, occur in a wide variety of situations. It is not always clear when these shifts are healthy and when they represent an illness. It is not always clear whether such shifts should be welcomed by Christians or should be resisted as spiritually dangerous. Consider the behaviour in the following description to discover what may be happening.[3]

> I see a large number of men and women, some sitting, some standing, some silent, others singing, others again talking apparently to themselves, and on coming closer we can make no sense of what they say. Some sway, others rock to and fro: some put their hands in the air and leave them there for some time. Others lie on the ground and roll around. I try to engage them in conversation but they seem to be in a private world of their own, quite unresponsive to conversation.

[3] The following section is based on material first published as Court, J. H. (1996), 'Discernment: Discerning between the emotional, the psychotic and the spiritual', *Renewal Journal*, 7, 1, 53–62. Reprinted here by permission.

What are we to make of these unusual kinds of behaviour? Is this sick, is it demonic, theatrical pretence, is it ecstatic? Is God being honoured, and if so, how can we know?

My picture is in fact a collage from experiences over the years. The description could be from my time working in the long-stay chronic wards of a psychiatric hospital before the new antipsychotic drugs arrived – the snake-pit days, still within living memory for some. The picture might be of a Balinese festival, with extended ceremonies, prayers and fire-walking. In this case we can also add a good deal of colour and music and flowers. The fire-walkers are impressive; whether due to trance or the help of some drugs, I cannot tell. The picture might also be that of a camp meeting with Rodney Howard-Browne, or the Toronto Blessing, but there, in addition to colour and music I would see many people on the ground and laughing uncontrollably. With these additions, we might also have been spectators in a large presentation of stage hypnosis by a skilled performer – a theatrical event in which these as well as other bizarre and unusual behaviours could be observed, strictly for entertainment.

My point in bringing these four possibilities together is that if we merely observe what is happening in a detached way, without a context, we shall witness a remarkable degree of similarity, but this will not answer the underlying questions of meaning. Seeking to sort experiences into the emotional *or* the psychotic *or* the spiritual by no means exhausts the categories of relevance. Emotion may be the product of something physiological, like a natural biochemical imbalance, or a drug trip. It may be more the product of interpersonal influences, such as openness to suggestion, persuasion and imitation. Spiritual experiences can, of course, also be subdivided by asking whether we are responding to a movement of the Spirit or to some demonic influence.

Less dramatically, we might observe a young boy with leukemia, who has to have frequent and painful injections as a part of his treatment. He remains surprisingly still as the doctor inserts a large needle into his spine, even though he has had no anaesthetic to help. Or we may watch the golfer as he stands on the green ready to putt, pausing for a few moments before he plays the stroke. He appears to be concentrating hard. Or the woman who has to attend the dentist for some serious root canal work, and sits back without any apparent distress, and again without anaesthetic. In these situations we can see hypnosis at work, helping people gain control of their experiences, so that they can deal better with their situation than they would otherwise.

Features of altered states of consciousness

Continuing to move towards what hypnosis is (and is not), the generic features of most ASCs will make it easier to put its special characteristics into perspective. There are a number of qualities which exist in hypnosis which are by no means unique, and hence the difficulty in defining where hypnosis starts and how it is distinct from other ASCs.[4]

1. Focused attention

This is a feature of most if not all ASCs which are actively sought out. Those who seek to use the experiences of yoga, transcendental meditation and similar states develop specific techniques to move from regular consciousness to the altered state. In a deliberate way attention is shifted away from surrounding events to become narrowly focused. This may involve moving attention inward to develop increased awareness of bodily sensations, or outward to attend in a focussed way on some external experience, to gaze at an object intently, or simply look at some chosen spot. The common theme is the restriction of perceptual input to become aware of as few extraneous experiences as possible.

This is also a feature of Christian meditative techniques. A deliberately quiet, non-intrusive environment is sought out and in that setting the mind is focused with the help of various spiritual exercises. In this context the focus is on the presence of God, but the process is similar. So too in hypnosis, regardless of the particular induction technique preferred, the intention is to withdraw from irrelevant distraction and achieve a state of highly focused attention. In this context, more than others, we commonly refer to entering a 'trance state', but this term is also used more widely ('I did it in a trance'; 'He was entranced by her beauty'), indicating how very similar the hypnotic experience is to many other common and powerful experiences. When used carefully, the term 'trance' refers to 'any state of mind in which the generalized reality-orientation has faded relatively to create a background awareness, which ignores what is going on around.'

Probably one of the commonest beliefs about hypnosis is that, to induce the state, there will be a swinging watch, or a strobe light used to capture and focus attention. While such external aids have been used for this purpose, they are far from essential, and indeed rarely used these days, as will be discussed further in Chapter 8.

---

4 See references in n. 2 above.

2. Repetition

Closely related to the focusing of attention, the use of repetition is a very widespread and powerful influence in bringing about an ASC. If we observe primitive religious experiences of ASCs, an obvious feature is the use of drumming and rhythm over extended periods. This will often be associated with the repetitive chanting of words or noises. The addition of rhythmic movement, as in dancing, waving arms, and swaying to the musical rhythm, can all enhance the impact of repetition. Such experiences produce an impact on central nervous system activity which, depending on the setting, may lead to increasing levels of excitement, or conversely to increasing depths of peaceful relaxation. Those who attend rock concerts can attest to the same kinds of effects. Repetition, rhythm and movement are major ingredients and, as with the religious ceremonies, words or sounds play a part – not so much to achieve meaning but rather to blot out links with logic and reason which would be distracting. In both settings this repetition is facilitated by anything which will enhance focused attention. Staring intently at one or more individuals can achieve eye focus and reduce awareness of how others around may be behaving. Reduced self-consciousness enables participants to engage freely in following the leader. In both settings, focus and repetition can be enhanced by the use of lighting – the flickering of a fire or the flashing of stage lights providing rhythm – and in both settings looking from a dark place towards the light ensures sustained focus.

In less action-packed settings the same principles can be applied. I still recall being admitted to the hospital at a young age for removal of my tonsils. As I waited to go into the operating room, the anaesthetist came up behind the barouche and placed a sweet-smelling pad over my nose and mouth, saying, 'Look at me and count backwards from ten.' He was using a task which focused my attention away from what was happening, and at the same time let him know when I had lost consciousness. I never reached the end of the count. Counting backwards is a task often used to help people enter hypnotic trance, as it requires careful attention, and serves to distract from whatever else may be happening.

3. Disruption of critical thought processes

The preceding examples incorporate the principle of moving away from rational, logical thought – which is a means we have of maintaining contact with reality – to think in a different way. Whether we begin to think in pictures and symbols, or our thinking becomes chaotically uncoordinated without any logical sequence, the result is the kind of shift that will induce an ASC.

One kind of shift from logical rationality is into 'primary process thinking'. This is a term favoured by psychoanalysts, and based on the Freudian theory that mental functioning is divided into id, ego and super-ego. Within these categories logical, conscious thought is associated with the ego and called a secondary process. The primary processes, associated with the functioning of the id, or unconscious, are non-rational and not constrained by time space reality. They are more characteristic of thinking among children than among adults.

A similar shift occurs as people abandon their sequential approach to knowledge, commonly said to be mediated by the brain's left hemisphere, in favour of a more discursive, freely associating and more symbolic kind of thinking, associated with right hemisphere activity.[5] While these two approaches are not mutually exclusive, and in normal brain functioning each can work with the other, there are measurable shifts of dominance in some altered states. The deliberate disruption of logical thinking is one of the intentions in brainwashing, in an attempt to get prisoners to change their mind-set to embrace alternative values and ideas.

Some have argued that, without any alterations of style, women are more at ease with thinking generated in the right hemisphere, resulting in ease with creativity, visual imagery and non-logical thought associations (sometimes termed 'women's ways of knowing'), whereas men are conditioned more towards the linear, logical, rational processes of the left hemisphere. While this difference may make it easier and more natural for women to adopt ASCs, there is no doubt that left and right brain activities are present in men and women, and both can choose to emphasize one or the other at any given time.

While the disruption of critical processes can occur in serious illness and in drug induced states, with severe disruption of functioning, a chosen shift into the creative use of imagery and visualization can be a richly rewarding experience. To be open to the experience of visions and to

---

[5] Gruzelier, J. & Warren, K. (1993), 'Neuropsychological evidence of reductions on left frontal tests with hypnosis', *Psychological Medicine, 23*, 93–101. Morgan C. M. (1979), 'Hypnotic susceptibility, EEG theta and alpha waves, and hemispheric specificity', in Burrows, G. D., Collison, D. R. & Dennerstein, L., (eds), *Hypnosis 1979: proceedings of the 8th International Congress of Hypnosis and Psychosomatic Medicine* (Amsterdam: Elsevier/North Holland Biomedical Press). Henninger, P. (1992) 'Conditional handedness: Handedness changes in multiple personality disordered subject reflect shift in hemispheric dominance', *Consciousness and Cognition, 1*, 265–287. Brown, P. (1991), *The hypnotic brain: hypnotherapy and social communication* (New Haven, CT: Yale University Press).

understand our world in different ways from usual may be a profoundly spiritual achievement[6]. Painters, sculptors and artists are often most at home with such ways of perceiving their world, and thereby achieve what others cannot imagine. Just because florid psychosis is also associated with unusual perceptions does not mean that all such differences should be rejected. One particular differentiation is the question of choice: do I choose the way I think (as with the artist), or do I think this way in spite of myself (as with the psychotic or the subject of brainwashing)?

Hypnosis is one of those ASCs in which non-rational thought is facilitated and critical judgment is actively discouraged in favour of the free-flowing activity associated with the right hemisphere of the brain. It follows that the experiences of trance may be expected to have much in common with the aesthetic world of art, imagery and dreams, and less to do with formal problem-solving. There is an openness to profound sensory experiences like visions or voices that acquire a closeness to reality which may make it hard to know where they came from. Used well, such experiences can be the basis for new understanding.

The idea that hypnosis involves a shift from left to right brain activity became popular in the 1970s and 80s, as electrophysiological evidence became available.[7] Conceptually, such positive findings of a shift gave strength to the view that hypnosis is a true ASC, and not a suggested response by subjects wanting to please the hypnotist. While this differentiation remains, it has become more complicated with further study. Crawford offers an analysis of such shifts and argues that highly hypnotizable people can best be described as cognitively flexible, that is, able to change cognitive strategies more readily than others, as well as showing hemisphere shifts.[8] This has been taken further to indicate that there are also shifts in function from the anterior to the posterior parts of the brain, coincidental with the left–right shift. This complexity of left–right and front–back obviously makes the picture more involved than the attractive simplicity a left-to-right shift suggested. Indeed it becomes even more complex when some offer evidence of a shift in focus away from the

---

[6] For an exploration across all the senses, see Roberts, A. O. (1996), *Messengers of God: The sensuous side of spirituality* (Newberg, OR: Barclay Press).

[7] Graham, K. R. (1977), 'Perceptual processes and hypnosis: support for a cognitive-state theory based on laterality', in Edmonston, W. E. (ed) *Conceptual and investigative approaches to hypnosis and hypnotic phenomena. Annals of New York Academy of Sciences, 296*, 274–83. Gruzelier & Warren, 'Neuropsychological evidence'. Morgan, 'Hypnotic susceptibility'.

[8] Crawford, H. J. (1989), 'Cognitive and physiological flexibility: multiple pathways to hypnotic responsiveness', in Ghorghin, V., Netter, P., Eysenck, H. & Rosenthal, R. (eds), *Suggestion and suggestibility: theory and research* (New York: Springer).

frontal to occipital cerebral activity,[9] while others contend for a shift to greater frontal activity in which the focus of attention enables richly creative experiences.[10] Left-right differences remain worthy of attention as we seek to understand hypnosis, but there is more to it.

4. *Use of imagery*

The interruption of logical thought processes may be completed by the facilitation of the non-logical processes associated with visualization and imagery. To the contemporary Western mind accustomed to thinking in scientific terms, logical thinking appears not only normative but also superior to alternatives. The scientific method rests on logical assumptions for the solution of problems, and the triumphs of science mean that this approach is highly prized.

It is not, however, the style of thinking that prevailed in earlier times in Western culture, nor is it universally favoured in Eastern cultures today. It is certainly not the preferred mode in the world of religious experience, nor is it the approach of the Bible. A significant feature of the science-versus-religion debate over the last two centuries has been the difficulty in deciding what constitutes evidence, and how we are to deal with subjective, inner experience. Science has favoured the rigour of experimentation, replication and objectivity. Evidences for religious experience are often not readily amenable to this approach and hence discarded by many scientists.

Nonetheless, there remains a strong current of belief in favour of phenomena which do not conveniently fit the demands of traditional scientific investigation. Within psychology, as within other sciences, there is a growing acceptance that inner experience, subjectivity, imagery and religious phenomena such as faith, can have legitimacy.[11]

The doctrinaire demands of scientific behaviourism, which insisted that only that which can be observed and measured is legitimate for study, are giving way to cognitive behaviourism which acknowledges mental processes and experiences (such things as beliefs and attitudes) to be important even when they cannot be directly observed. Even the strong tradition of logical positivism in psychology is coming under challenge in favour of other ways of knowing.[12]

---

[9] ibid.

[10] e.g. Walter, H. (1992), *Hypnose: Theorien, neurophysiologische Korrelate und praktische Hinweise* (Stuttgart: Thieme).

[11] Schorr, J. E. (1983), *Psychotherapy through imagery* (New York: Theime-Stratton)

[12] Josselon, R. & Lieblich, A. (1996) 'Fettering the mind in the name of "science" ' *American Psychologist, 51*, 6, 651–6.

As a result, the phenomena of ASCs can now be studied instead of being simply dismissed as pre-scientific nonsense. Dreams, visions, and intuitions, for example, have long been held in high regard in most cultures. Imagery, as the deliberate use of a pictorial way of thinking and experiencing an inner reality, is nothing new and, indeed, is taken for granted in many cultures. The biblical tradition is particularly strong in using and valuing imagery. The linguistic style of metaphor and allusion runs through the entire record, as the natural vehicle of communication for Middle-Eastern readers before the advent of modern science. The content similarly is rich with dreams and visions which are taken to be authentic experiences with spiritual significance. This tradition is being rediscovered by professional therapists in their use of story telling as a powerful vehicle for healing.

Hypnosis, in common with other ASCs, is characterized by the rich use of imagery and the use of images is often deliberately facilitated both to enhance the hypnotic state itself, and as a vehicle for bringing about desired changes. It is ironic that, as scientific psychology has moved in recent years away from worshipping scientific objectivity as the ideal approach to knowledge, to embrace ways of knowing more commonly espoused by the religious traditions, we should find voices of protest from Christian writers such as Dave Hunt,[13] who would condemn the use of visualization imagery as somehow anti-biblical and spiritually dangerous. The scaremongering approach of these authors has led to rebuttals by many Christians, and a direct confrontation, on a biblical basis, was published under the title *Seduction?? A biblical response.*[14]

The deliberate enhancement of imagery is, of course, nothing quantitatively different from everyday experience. We all frequently think in pictures. We remember the past with the help of visual memories. Our world is enriched by auditory memories of voices, music, etc. which are often then linked to visual recall. Our spiritual experience would be extremely limited if governed only by words and propositions. We have only to ask 'What is God like?' to find that, for most people, God is represented in some form of mental imagery. To say 'God is love' may be a profound statement but it does not generate the kind of response that comes from a picture representing the qualities we associate with God. From time immemorial, religious beliefs have been expressed

---

[13] Hunt, D. & McMahon, T. A. (1985), *The seduction of Christianity* (Eugene, OR: Harvest House).

[14] Reid, T. F., Vicker, M., Laine, J. A. & Langstaff, A. (1986), *Seduction?? A biblical response* (New Wilmington, PA: Son-Rise Publications).

visually – from cave-paintings to stained glass windows, from Michelangelo's Sistine Chapel to contemporary art and films.

Imagery and visualization are central components of the way we understand our world. If we can find ways of doing this better, that is likely to be valuable. In the various ASCs it does become possible to enhance these processes. This engagement in right-hemisphere thinking is a significant feature in the shift from the external world to inner awareness.

5. Passivity

Most of us live in an active mode. That is, we are busy doing, we act on our world to make things happen, we understand the aphorism 'We work to live' (while others prefer 'We live to work'), and even when not working we commonly enjoy active leisure pursuits such as sports.

By contrast, there is what is often called the passive mode (though the term 'receptive' better captures the alert acceptance of information in a state which is more that simply resting). In this state we do not seek to initiate but rather to respond. In the passive mode we receive stimulation and process it. The artist may find the need to wait for inspiration (passive) before being able to produce the work of art (active). The reader of a thriller may simply be led along to the final disclosure (passive) or work to find the clues to solve the mystery before the end (active). The Christian tradition is enriched by its emphasis on waiting on God.

It is characteristic of the ASCs that they are predominantly passive. Anaesthesia for surgery is an extreme example of being acted upon by others, while needing to adopt a passive role. When people use the leisure drugs they cannot determine what the effect will be but have to wait and find out. A bad trip is not chosen but something that comes to the recipient involuntarily. Even when we are tired and need sleep we know that we can try too hard with negative results. The experiences of relaxation, meditation and trance are all entered most successfully by those who allow things to happen, rather than trying hard to enter them.

While passivity is predominant, it is important to stress that this is not to the exclusion of activity. There are choices to be made, techniques may be employed, and the altered state may allow inter-activity. The person who becomes drunk may become very active, and great debate surrounds the extent to which drunks are responsible for their actions. Some may wish to argue that they are totally at the mercy of the effects of alcohol and cannot be held responsible for their actions (defence lawyers favour this view) but most people recognize that some degree of choice remains. A more compelling case is made when someone who suffers from schizophrenia, or is under the influence of drugs producing a similar state, experiences a powerful hallucination and then acts as if this false perception were a reality. The experience of unwelcome sights, sounds, voices, and feelings are examples of the passivity endured by those in a seriously altered state.

In the voluntarily chosen states such as meditation and relaxation, it is clear that the capacity for choice remains, and when an unfamiliar experience occurs and is passively received, then the active response to this can be chosen. It is not so immediately obvious that the same is true for the hypnotic trance state, so one of the most common beliefs is that people will be under the complete power of another, and unable to resist doing things they would refuse to do at other times. That is, a popular view of hypnosis is one of total passivity and loss of control. This possibility deserves more extended discussion, and will be raised again in Chapter 8.

6. Trusting relationship

Not all ASCs involve relating to someone else. Some forms of meditation and yoga, for example, are practised privately and emphasize an entirely personal experience. Others involve not a human relationship but an encounter with God. Christian meditation may be practised in a solitary setting, but it specifically seeks a relationship with God.

Many ASCs involve an interaction with another person who is in some way instrumental in the process. Anaesthesia and hypnosis are two clear examples where the altered state involves another person, and both usually assume a good deal of trust. The attitude of passivity and receptivity is most successful when it is undertaken safely. Hypnosis is found to be readily induced, other things being equal, when there is trust and confidence in the hypnotist.

Trusting another person enough to be willing to go into an altered state is a major commitment, not to be undertaken lightly. We do this most readily when we feel safe with that other person, when we believe they will act ethically and responsibly, when we believe them to have the necessary skills for the task, and when we share the same basic values. While such considerations may be less important for anaesthesia (which is an adjunct to surgery, and the trust issue relates to all involved in the procedure), they are of great significance for hypnosis. They bear on the questions of how safe hypnosis is and to whom we should entrust ourselves. This will receive further examination in Chapter 8.

7. *Heightened suggestibility*

It follows from several of the features already mentioned that people in an ASC will commonly be more open to ideas, to persuasion and to influence than they would be at other times. Brainwashing techniques specifically seek to bring about changes that will enable new attitudes and beliefs to be implanted with conviction. Under more relaxing conditions, suggestibility can also be heightened due to a relaxation of the normal level of vigilance. When we are normally alert we scan incoming information carefully, and so avoid being misled or duped. Similarly, we protect ourselves from any potential threat. With changing states of consciousness, we may be caught off-guard, and accept input which at other times would be rejected. Lowered vigilance can be a pre-cursor for heightened suggestibility. A more relaxed physiological state can be part of this lowered vigilance, including a change in the level of cortical arousal. Our brains work within a careful balance of opposing mechanisms, known as inhibition and excitation, designed to preserve a stable state. In the hypnotic experience this balance moves in favour of reduced inhibition, and a greater openness to ideas.

Such changes occurring in hypnosis, along with the passively receptive state which is common, mean that it is possible to tell the person in trance things they would at other times find hard to believe, and yet they will accept with a kind of suspended disbelief. Usually if someone is told 'Your arm has become very light and it will float freely in the air' they will not accept this suggestion, yet this is readily accepted as possible in hypnotic situations. Not only is the possibility accepted, but it happens readily for most people who observe the effect with interest and amazement, as if it were happening to someone else.

To be in a state of heightened suggestibility is to be at risk from any unscrupulous person who might seek to exploit the situation. This is a danger to be acknowledged. On the other hand, there are many situations where we would like to be able to believe and experience, yet have difficulty in doing so. If the person living with chronic pain can find a way to ignore it, or reduce it, or relocate it with the help of suggestion, this can be a great blessing.

The most commonly expressed concern related to this shift in suggestibility in trance is that one will accept the suggestion to engage in embarrassing or immoral behaviour, which would be rejected under other circumstances. This fear, which comes primarily from what occurs in stage hypnosis, will be given further attention in Chapter 8.

8. Physiological changes

Among the most striking and dramatic features of ASCs are the changes in physical sensation and performance which can occur. These changes are so great as to be almost unbelievable at times, fearsome at others, and a source of great benefit in clinical settings. We are not surprised these days, though perhaps we should be, when patients undergo major surgery lasting many hours sustaining physical interventions which, prior to anaesthesia, would have been impossible. Similarly a visit to the dentist has become a great deal less fear-provoking thanks to local anaesthesia. It remains astonishing to discover that a woman can experience labour and even a Caesarian section without pain, thanks to hypnosis. It is remarkable when major oral surgery is undertaken without any help other than hypnosis.

There are many well-documented examples from the East of yogis who have learned to control, through meditation, the bodily regulating systems, known as the autonomic nervous system, thereby bringing about amazing changes in basic physiological activity, without experiencing any harm. One example is a Hindu who in 1970, through the practice of yoga, was able to remain in a sealed metal box for over five hours. His experience was studied closely, and it was found that he was able to survive using only just over half of the estimated minimum oxygen needed to sustain life.[15] In such ASCs it appears that the messages to the regulatory parts of the brain can be modified, thereby achieving what seems otherwise impossible. At the other end of the energy scale, we know that psychotics can develop enormous strength requiring several people to restrain them. When people are drunk or on drugs their tolerance for pain and their persistent activity can go well beyond normal limits. Similarly, we know of remarkable feats of heroism associated with strength performed by mothers when their children are at risk.

Clearly, there are physiological resources available to us well beyond the limits we take as normal. Tapping into these greater resources can be of immense value and, as usual with something so powerful, they can also be highly dangerous if not used responsibly. Those who regularly push

---

[15] Gross, R. D. (1993), *Psychology: the science of mind and behaviour* (London: Hodder and Stoughton), pp. 124–5.

the limits of endurance, like Olympic athletes, know that there is a level of functioning which represents the upper limit beyond which they cannot – ordinarily – go. However, that limit can be pushed back under some circumstances, and hypnosis is widely used to assist in this.[16]

The closest physiological links these days with hypnosis are states achieved through meditation and relaxation. Indeed, it is often difficult if not impossible to distinguish between these objectively. The pursuit of a calm, relaxed and focused state is common to them all and many therapists who claim to teach relaxation techniques are actually inducing a hypnotic trance state without even realizing it. Others, including Christian therapists, recognize that they are using hypnotic phenomena but prefer to avoid the term 'hypnosis' because of its negative connotations.

However, it does not follow that the hypnotic trance state is always one of peaceful relaxation. Those who have witnessed demonstrations of stage hypnosis know that there can be a great deal of activity and energy in stage performances and, without this, there will be little audience interest. So, too, in earlier days, when Mesmer began to use his animal magnetism (later known as mesmerism, and then hypnosis) his patients were far from tranquil and relaxed. He deliberately set out to induce major reactions of a quite dramatic kind as an essential part of his treatments.

> Responses varied also among people as a function of their previous experiences. . . . For the more experienced patients, there were different types of reaction. Some would laugh, sweat, yawn, shiver. . . They shouted, cried, fell asleep or lost consciousness. They sweated profusely. Laughter and shivers became convulsive. In all this, Mesmer appeared like the conductor of an orchestra.[17]

He was inducing physiological changes, though different from those preferred today. What links the two very different kinds of response is the fact that subjects respond to the hypnotist's expectations. Through hyper-suggestibility one hypnotist can expect and produce convulsions as readily as another can expect and produce states of deep peacefulness. This observation leads naturally to a final general point.

---

[16] e.g. L.-E. Uneståhl working with Swedish athletes. See his monograph (1981) *New paths of sport learning and excellence* (Örebro: University Dept of Sport Psychology, Örebro). See also Morgan, W. P. (1993), 'Hypnosis and sport Psychology' in Rhue, J. W., Lynn, S. J., & Kirsch, I. (eds), *Handbook of clinical hypnosis* (Washington, DC: American Psychological Association).

[17] Laurence, J. R. & Perry, C. (1988), *Hypnosis, will and memory: A psycho-legal history* (New York: Guilford), p. 59.

9. Demand characteristics

Demand characteristics is a technical term referring to the expectations placed on us. When we feel some sense of expectation or even obligation to respond to suggestions we are in demand situation. The hypnotic experience is one in which there is high demand to respond, and the way the trance is experienced will be greatly influenced both by what the hypnotist is expecting, and by what the person in trance expects to happen. As a result, one of the difficulties in defining ASCs, and especially hypnotic states, is that they vary so much. Not only are there large individual differences such that some achieve changes more readily than others. In addition, the expectations a person has of what will happen, combined with the expectations of the person involved in producing the change, can result in effects so varied that it is difficult to see them all related to trance.

This difference is not unlike the effects that alcohol can have on drinkers. There are those who on getting drunk become so slowed that they go into a deep sleep, whereas others behave very differently, becoming aggressive and vocal. The same drug is producing strikingly different responses. In religious rituals there are wide varieties of behaviour associated with the altered states produced by rhythm, dance and repetition (with or without mood-altering drugs), but within particular cultures or religious groups there is a great deal of similarity. Fire-walking in one place, snake-handling in another, suggest that the behaviour arises from expectations of the participants, and these come from the demand characteristics of those around them.

Since hypnosis is so widely practised, there are many different expectations associated with the trance state. Some expect to go into a sleep-like state because they are told this will happen – and they do. Others are told they will not remember anything that occurs in the trance state after it is past – and sure enough, amnesia, partial or complete, occurs. A major problem can arise when people are instructed to recall elements from an earlier event, such as a crime or an accident, and then claim to be able to do so. It is not easy to distinguish true from false recall. Even more striking memories can occur when someone is instructed to recall in trance events from past lives – and many memories are produced which appear to confirm that the person has had one or several previous lives. Such memories do not provide support for reincarnation, but they do emphasize the strength of demand characteristics.

The expectations placed on people, either deliberately or inadvertently, contribute to the ongoing debate about the validity of memories of past abuse. Memories of the past retrieved while in hypnosis are highly susceptible to the expectations of the therapist, such that serious doubts are often raised about their validity. These phenomena need to be reviewed in the light of this concept of demand characteristics. The hypnotist can find what is being looked for, whether grounded in reality or not. This effect has significant implications both psychologically (e.g. 'Can we believe what people claim to remember?') and theologically (e.g. 'What are we to make of reports of reincarnation?'). For further treatment of these questions see Chapters 3 and 8, and Appendix 1.

Summary

A number of features found in altered states of consciousness have been identified in order to establish that there are many such states, and we all have experience of some of them. There are states which are chosen while others are involuntary. They can be facilitated, and a number of the methods for achieving ASCs have been described. Those who seek to induce an ASC in themselves or in others typically apply several of these methods to converge and be mutually supportive. The results vary, with a few people rarely experiencing any altered states, while a small percentage have a great facility for entering ASCs.

Hypnosis can be understood as one among these many states and we have good evidence that people can be arranged according to their ability to enter a hypnotic state, i.e. their hypnotizability. We have not yet achieved a definition which would differentiate hypnosis as a recognizable state in some way different from others. This will be attempted in the next chapter. In anticipation of this, it is worth making one negative statement: hypnosis is not sleep. While it is commonly a sleep-like state, and the word hypnosis itself suggests sleep (derived from the Greek word for sleep), this is another area of popular confusion which needs to be pursued more fully.

Chapter 2

What is Hypnosis?

Circling around the meaning of hypnosis by considering similar and related states makes it possible to consider how to define it. It becomes evident that there will be several definitions rather than one, because it has so many applications and such a long history. It may also emerge that, when defined, hypnosis is not at all what is popularly supposed. Its chequered history, its misuse and its mystique all lead to misunderstanding which needs to be corrected if we are to give it fair consideration.

Hypnosis is not sleep

When I teach students, I sometimes set the scene for a definition by referring to Paul's words in 1 Corinthians 15, 'Behold, I show you a mystery. We shall not all sleep, but we shall all be changed: In a moment, in the twinkling of an eye. . .' With this introduction several key points can be made.

'Behold!' A commanding verb calls for attention to the speaker. Hypnosis typically involves the capture and holding of a person's attention. Usually, but not necessarily, it will be by eye-contact looking at some place or object in a fixed manner. Traditional methods of hypnotic induction have included instructions such as 'Pay close attention to my watch', in the days when a fob-watch was swung rhythmically; or 'Look deep into my eyes', and a sustained stare was produced as a means of holding a person's attention. Commonly today, subjects are instructed to look intently at a spot at some distance which by virtue of eye-fatigue becomes blurred. The common element is capturing and holding attention.

'I show you a mystery.' The reference to a mystery in the New Testament is to that which is not widely understood, but revealed to an initiated

group. It can be readily adapted to the concept of hypnosis. It is to many people a mystery in the more general sense that they are intrigued by hypnosis but only vaguely understand it. But it also qualifies as a mystery in the New Testament sense, as something best understood through careful instruction to those who take a particular interest in it, thereby becoming initiated. Hypnosis is not something to be taken lightly or used casually without awareness of its potential power. In religious and in therapeutic settings there is usually some kind of qualifying procedure leading to the induction of those intending to practise.

'*We shall not all sleep.*' In the Corinthians passage the use of the term 'sleep' is clearly a euphemism for death, and refers to the Christian hope of the second coming of Christ. It is the same term (ὕπυοζ) which forms the root of the word 'hypnotism', and which was coined by Dr James Braid in 1843 because the state was considered a sleep-like condition ('hypnotism' has, over the years, been replaced by 'hypnosis', even though Braid later regretted the term's suggestion of a sleep-like state). Sleep-like it may be, but it is no more sleep than is death. As indicated in the previous chapter, a person who is in hypnosis can be focused, attentive, responsive to suggestion, and have clear recall later of all that occurs during that period. When we add that it is possible to move around, speak, and carry out various tasks as requested, it is clearly not sleep-like in all respects.

The same sentence, 'we shall not all sleep', provides another helpful reminder, that while most people are hypnotizable, a small percentage do not respond under normal circumstances. If we follow the evidence derived from various standard tests which are sometimes used, we might conclude that around ten per cent of people are not responsive, while another ten per cent are very highly hypnotizable, with the majority fitting in between. However, when it comes to actually seeking a trance state, those who are willing and who work with a skilled hypnotist almost always achieve some level of trance. Most practitioners agree that there are those suffering from psychosis and from mental impairment who are not responsive. On the other hand, those who vigorously proclaim 'I cannot be hypnotized' are often surprised, since with a skilled practitioner it is possible to overcome the resistance based on ignorance, fear or pride, and achieve a cooperation that ensures a good level of trance.

'*But we shall all be changed.*' This is a glorious promise of ultimate salvation. In this life, no such promises are warranted, but we do acknowledge both the desirability and possibility of many kinds of change. We all struggle with the kind of dilemma that Paul expressed in Romans 7:15, 'I do not understand what I do. For what I want to do I do not do, but what I hate I do.' That spiritual struggle is also experienced as a psychological tension as we seek to find ways of behaving that are congruent with what we know to be right. The desire for change drives people to seek help in many directions, and it is evident that some degree of success is often achieved, even if it is short-lived and suffers relapse. The dramatic benefits from surgery and medication encourage belief in the medical profession as a major source of healing change. The life-changing experience of Christian conversion is sufficient to assure us that real change can occur and be long-lasting. The psychological professions also claim to help people change and are, to varying degrees, successful. Many other healing groups exist, and continue to do so because they have followers who attest to the benefits. We need not doubt that change is possible for all. How much, of what kind, and for how long, are the disputed questions.

Hence, in relation to hypnosis, we can confidently say change is possible. For some this may be only minimal, but for others the change can be dramatic, beneficial and long-standing. The concern for Christians, then, is not whether hypnosis is associated with change but, since it is, whether it will be for good or ill. Is it to be seen as more allied with the beneficial changes that arise from spiritual conversion or good medicine or is it, as some fear, more akin to the dangerous changes of the occult? In addition, for the person considering hypnosis as an approach to change, a further question is whether such change will be transitory or maintained (see Chapter 8).

'*In a moment, in the twinkling of an eye.*' One of the most common beliefs of those seeking healing through hypnotic techniques is that the results will be instantaneous. Especially amongst those with habit disorders such as smoking or over-eating the approach is commonly, 'I've had the problem for years. I've tried everything else. I am expecting a one-session instant cure.' The thinly veiled agenda is that the therapist is expected to achieve this remarkable outcome, while anything less is a failure for the therapist. This scenario is a formula for frustration and anger since it is based on false assumptions. As we shall see below, change, when it occurs, arises from the person seeking change at least as much as from anything a therapist may do or say. It is naive to suppose that long established patterns of behaviour will be suddenly and irreversibly changed through one experience. Of course, people in distress want to believe this will occur. Unfortunately, some charlatans have fostered this belief using those unusual examples where dramatic change is achieved quickly, in order to suggest that it is typical. The basis for change can be established in a moment, but in those areas where hypnosis is therapeutic, were typically concerned with patterns of behaviour, attitudes and physiological responses where gradual change occurs.

There is here a close parallel with the inner healing movement in the church. While it is always exciting to hear stories of instant and dramatic healings associated with prayer, it would be misleading to believe that this is the only kind of spiritual healing possible. Nor should we assume that all such healings continue without relapse over time. The reality for both hypnosis and inner healing work is that sometimes quite striking change occurs dramatically and suddenly, but most often benefits arise following sustained periods of time. In both settings, relapses also occur.

Some attempts to define hypnosis

This is perhaps the most challenging question addressed in this book. It is possible to find definitions in textbooks, and a few will be offered here, but three things are clear. Firstly, there is no universally agreed definition. Secondly, it is a great deal easier to say what it is not (hence the first section of this chapter). Thirdly, there are even those who will maintain that it does not exist at all, so there is nothing to define.

Assuming that hypnosis does exist, most definitions are confined to two or three lines. For example, the distinguished experimental psychologist, Ernest Hilgard, suggests:

> the state of consciousness caused in a subject by a systematic procedure for altering consciousness, usually carried out by one person (the hypnotist) to alter the consciousness of another (the subject).[1]

Hilgard has contributed very substantially to the scientific understanding of what hypnosis is and how it works, and has placed particular emphasis on the importance of dissociation, and seeing hypnosis as an ASC.

The importance of suggestibility as a key element in the hypnotic experience comes through in a definition offered by Rubin and McNeil:

> an altered state of consciousness, in which the hypnotized subject can be influenced to behave and to experience things differently than she would in the ordinary waking state.[2]

The Penguin dictionary of psychology departs from its usual brief format to provide a more extended and helpful reference for hypnosis:

---

1 Hilgard, E. R. (1975), 'Hypnosis', *Annual Review of Psychology, 26*, 19–44.

2 Rubin, Z. & McNeil, E. B. (1983), *The psychology of being human* (New York: Harper and Row).

> Few terms in the psychological lexicon are so thoroughly wrapped in mysticism and confusion. The problems arise from the tendency that dates back to the discoverer, Franz Anton Mesmer (1733–1815), to regard the process of hypnotism as one which transports the subject into a separate state of mind. Further complication emerged because the phenomenon attracted a coterie of charlatans, faith healers and, more recently, night-club entertainers who make unsubstantiated claims and show a singular reluctance to use proper controls in their work.[3]

After describing features of the hypnotic state, this description remarks that

> All of these effects are of a kind, in that they are also characteristic of a normal person who has voluntarily given up conscious control, a person who evidences extreme suggestibility.[4]

Encompassed within those explanatory remarks, five key elements are identified by Reber:

> (a) Although it superficially resembles a sleep-like state, the EEG pattern does not resemble any of the stages of sleep; (b) Normal planning functions are reduced, a hypnotized person tends to wait passively for instructions from the hypnotist; (c) Attention becomes highly selective, the individual may hear only one person to the exclusion of others; (d) Role-playing is readily accomplished; (e) Post-hypnotic suggestion is often observed, frequently a specific amnesia where the subject cannot recall things he or she has been told to forget.[5]

An earlier definition, constituted by the British Medical Association to give credibility to its use by medical practitioners, referred to

> a temporary condition of altered attention in the subject which may be induced by another person and in which a variety of phenomena may appear spontaneously or in response to verbal or other stimuli. These phenomena include alterations in the subject of responses and ideas unfamiliar to him in his usual state of mind. Further, phenomena such as anaesthesia, paralysis and rigidity of muscles, and vasomotor changes can be produced and removed in the hypnotic state.[6]

This definition was invoked by David Collison, a Christian psychiatrist, when addressing his professional colleagues in his Presidential Address to the Australian Society of Hypnosis.[7] Among secular professionals bold enough to attempt a definition, Araoz says, more briefly:

---

[3] Reber, G. (1985), *The Penguin dictionary of psychology* (Harmondsworth: Penguin), p. 334.

[4] ibid. pp. 334–5.

[5] ibid.

[6] *British Medical Journal* (1955), quoted in Collison, D. R. (1990), 'A visit to Cos: In search of origins and traditions', *Australian Journal of Clinical and Experimental Hypnosis*, *18*, 2, 63–70.

[7] See n. 6.

> Hypnosis is a state in which the critical mental faculties are temporarily suspended and the person uses mainly imagination or primary-process thinking.[8]

These last two definitions come from the tradition of therapy concerned with the importance of thought processes in the development of disorders. They assume that accessing the 'deeper' mental processes of the unconscious is a valuable way of enabling change at the conscious, or secondary, level, and follow in the psychoanalytic tradition which argues that much of what we seek to do is adversely affected by mechanisms such as repression and dissociation, so that therapy is directed to circumventing these mechanisms.

Since there still remains in many people's minds the idea of hypnosis as a mystique, something dramatically different from everyday experience, we should add two further comments from contemporary respected professionals. D. Corydon Hammond places hypnosis squarely in the area of communication stating that

> Hypnosis is the art of securing a patient's attention and then effectively communicating ideas that enhance motivation and change perceptions.[9]

Such a definition is so broad that the first word might well be replaced by education, therapy or even evangelism. A similarly non-threatening definition is proposed by the authors Alman and Lambrou who, in writing about self-hypnosis, propose that

> Hypnosis is a phenomenon characterized by an individual's increased openness to acceptable suggestions while in a state of heightened and focused concentration.[10]

There is then, in contemporary definitions, a recognition that hypnosis is more than a passive state of receptivity. Rather, it provides a special context for communication whereby selected thoughts, ideas and beliefs can be changed. It can be the vehicle for education and re-education. This is the task for psychotherapists more generally, as well as for preachers. This interpersonal stance is adopted by Michael Yapko who says:

> The essence of what I am discussing here is communication and interpersonal influence, and that is precisely where hypnosis comes in. . . Somewhere in the communications of both the hypnotist and the psychotherapist are specific components that enable a client's subjective experience to be altered and

---

[8] Araoz, D. L. (1982), *Hypnosis and sex therapy* (New York: Brunner/Mazel), p.9.

[9] Hammond D. C. (1990), *Handbook of hypnotic suggestions and metaphors* (New York: W.W. Norton), p. 2.

[10] Alman, B. M. & Lambrou, P. (1992), *Self-hypnosis* (New York: Brunner/ Mazel), p. 276.

therapeutic influence to take place. Approaching hypnosis from this interactional standpoint places emphasis on being an effective communicator.[11]

Attempts by Christians to define hypnosis

In addition to these descriptive definitions from practitioners, we must also recognize that some Christian writers have provided definitions and interpretations, sometimes with a very different emphasis. A positive interpretation has been provided by George Matheson who, writing deliberately for a Christian audience in the *Baker encyclopedia of psychology*, proposes that

> Hypnosis appears to involve a shift in concentration, executed in a passive manner (such as occurs in daydreaming or sleeping), resulting in a state of consciousness distinguishably different from alertness or ordinary sleep. It is characterized by narrowing of attention, reduced rational criticalness, and increased responsiveness to suggestion. It appears to provide clearer access to the functioning of the mind, allowing access to that which is subconscious or dissociated. Additionally, it seems to play a role as a mediator or transducer between cognitive and physiological functioning.[12]

On the other hand, Christian writers have often issued strong warnings to their readers, and these concerns will be discussed in Chapters 7 and 8, since this requires a consideration of various interpretations of the hypnotic experience and of the meaning of relevant biblical passages.

The recognition of significant benefits in a Christian context, while acknowledging hazards, is now clear in professional journals[13] as well as in books written for Christian audiences.[14] This move towards increasing acceptance of hypnosis as a legitimate aid to therapy is paralleled by the trend within the professional literature, where for many years hypnotic approaches were often viewed with scepticism but have now been embraced within mainstream practice. Considering the very long history of hypnosis in various forms over many centuries, it has taken a long time to move out of the shadows. This is not altogether surprising in view of

---

[11] Yapko, M. D. (1995), *Essentials of hypnosis* (New York: Brunner/Mazel).

[12] Matheson, G. (1985), 'Hypnosis', in Benner, D. G. (ed), *Baker encyclopedia of psychology* (Grand Rapids, MI: Baker Book House), p.552.

[13] e.g. Matheson, G. (1979), 'Hypnotic aspects of religious experiences', *Journal of Psychology and Theology*, 7, 1, 13–21.

[14] Morton, R. B. (1980), *Hypnosis and pastoral counseling* (Los Angeles, CA: Westwood Publishing); Matheson, 'Hypnotic aspects of religious experiences'; Court, J. H. (1991), 'Lord of the trance', *Journal of Psychology and Christianity, 10*, 3, 261–5.

the abuses and misunderstandings that have occurred. The famous psychologist Clark Hull wrote in 1933: 'All sciences alike have descended from magic and superstition, but none has been so slow as hypnosis in shaking off the evil association of its origin.'[15]

A historical footnote to this more recent transition is in order here. Rather ahead of his time, and responding to concerns expressed by Christians, Don Tweedie, then on the faculty of Fuller Seminary, wrote in 1963 about his own experience as a Christian who practised hypnosis. After hearing the objections to hypnosis expressed many times, he wrote: 'Evangelical Christians have been rather slow to embrace this long presumed demonic device, and are often quite assured that it is somehow contrary to Christian morals. Hypnosis is occasionally asserted to be a state of demonic oppression, or, at a minimum, the usurpation of the prerogatives of God to try to attain control over another person.'[16] He describes a number of personal experiences of Christians speaking strongly against hypnosis, and concludes that 'Superstition is not confined to Christians or lay groups concerning hypnosis . . . Most of the negative reaction to hypnosis is based upon an almost absolute ignorance of it as a process and a complete lack of first hand information'.[17] He gives his own account of how hypnotic work can be incorporated into therapy conducted within a Christian framework, pointing to positive possibilities while cautioning against its use to bring people to a personal decision about Jesus Christ.

Written so long ago, Tweedie's comments have apparently passed almost unnoticed, so they deserve recapitulation as a good exposition of the limits and benefits to be observed. A discussion of religious experiences is pertinent, however, and, in suggesting decision options for a psychotherapy patient, suggestions to consider God's will are just as appropriate as any other suggestions. Murray's comment on hypnosis closely approximates my own opinion:

> Such suggestion is no implantation, as many think, of an alien and unnecessary element into the personality. Religious suggestion is as potent and as necessary to the full expression and development of that personality as any other, and has as much right to be given. Nevertheless, one stipulation, peculiar to the Christian system, must be made. Religion is built up from two influences, man's desire and God's power. We can but educate and release the first; we cannot command the second. Therefore, it is illegitimate to suggest to a man under hypnosis, 'When you wake up, you will believe in Christ'; that is altogether outside our province,

---

15 Hull, C. (1933), *Hypnosis and suggestibility* (New York: Grove Press).
16 Tweedie, D. F. (1963) *The Christian and the couch: An introduction to Christian logotherapy* (Grand Rapids, MI: Baker Book House), p. 169.
17 ibid. p. 170.

> and in God's. What we can and ought to do, is so to open up his mind, so to give play to his religious instinct, so to clear the channels, that a new perception of God's presence may do the rest.[18]

To bear witness in as psychologically positive circumstance as possible is but to follow in the way of the Holy Spirit. We need to remember, however, that healing decisions are to be free, clear and responsible decisions, made by sufferers for themselves.

> Hypnosis is a very helpful technique in a Christian psychotherapy. In the hands of the competent therapist it can be an amazing ally in the guidance of the therapeutic process. Ill-considered objections, on the grounds of Christian ethics, previously have delayed the full utilization of hypnosis, but new understanding, and the increasing acceptance of it in the scientific community, augurs well for this method in the advancement of Christ's Kingdom in the field of psychotherapy.[19]

Stage hypnosis

Clark Hull's reference to the practice of hypnosis as a descent from magic introduces another reason for diverse views about its nature. Whereas most of the current scientific literature refers to the use of hypnosis as part of a healing process (hypnotherapy), and Christian writers have largely emphasized the dangers associated with its use in occult practices, there is a third area where hypnosis is highly visible, i.e. stage hypnosis. This is a special case in which the appearance of magic is strong. This is often the only experience people have of hypnosis, through seeing a show live or on television.

The stage use of hypnotic techniques as entertainment is sufficiently different in style and purpose from its clinical use to deserve separate consideration. Exposure to stage hypnosis, and amateur displays at parties, colours people's view of what to expect if hypnotherapy is recommended. I was once consulted by a mother and her teenage daughter together, who had been told hypnosis could help with their respective problems. When asked about their prior knowledge or experience of hypnosis they said they had recently seen a stage presentation. Both attended the same performance, yet, when I asked how it affected the thought of experiencing hypnosis themselves, they had opposite reactions. The mother said

---

18 Murray, J. A. C. (1947), *An introduction to a Christian psychotherapy* (Edinburgh: T and T. Clark), p.233.

19 Tweedie, *The Christian and the couch*, pp. 172–3.

she was afraid she would be told to do embarrassing or silly things, so it was with some reluctance she agreed to attend. The daughter reported being most impressed with the dramatic effects she had seen and this had persuaded her such power could help her overcome her problem.

Neither had been exposed to the clinical approach to hypnosis, and maybe neither had even seen hypnosis used at all! The fact is that, while stage hypnotists are highly skilled in knowing and using the phenomena of altered states, and deliberately focus a good deal on the behavioural signs which appear to demonstrate the hypnotic state, much of what happens is closer to the stage presentation of the magician or illusionist. (I prefer the latter term in order to avoid the occultic implications of the term 'magic', which are quite unwarranted in stage entertainments by magicians. Magic, as referred to here, is 'the professed art of performing wonders by using misdirection of attention'.[20])

Clinicians are taught that whatever can be achieved in hypnosis can also be achieved out of hypnosis. So too the stage entertainer knows that a hypnotic trance is not required for the feats that are demonstrated. Certainly such shows are enhanced by careful selection of performers who demonstrate high suggestibility on preliminary tests (like being told to clasp their hands tightly, and then having difficulty separating them). Subjects who have shown themselves to be cooperative and suggestible are likely to go into trance because of the demand characteristics of the situation, but this is not necessary. Much of the drama is generated by getting the performers to do things they did not know they could do (and attributing the results to a deep trance state), combined with an audience carefully prepared and led along to believe in the appearances as a result of skilful showmanship.

One of the commonest and most convincing stage demonstrations is to place a man horizontally between two chairs with his head on one, feet on the other, and unsupported between. The apparent rigidity of a wooden plank impresses the audience, and this may be enhanced if a pretty girl is then invited to stand on his chest. Very impressive! Yet it has been shown that almost anyone can achieve suspension like this for two to three minutes without hypnosis, and that when a man is suspended like this he can support a weight of 300 pounds without difficulty.[21]

Combining such effects with clever patter, illusions and planting ideas

---

[20] Kroger, W. S. (1977), *Clinical and experimental hypnosis* (Philadelphia: Lippincott), p. 129.

[21] Collins J. K. (1961), 'Muscular endurance in normal and hypnotic states: A study suggested catalepsy', quoted in Zilbergeld, B., Edelstein, M. G. & Araoz, D. L. (eds) (1986), *Hypnosis: Questions and Answers* (New York: W. W. Norton), p. 26.

within the minds of observers can produce a remarkably effective show. Some see this as an abuse of hypnosis and potentially harmful to those who may feel deceived or cheated. Others consider it as largely irrelevant to the clinical use of hypnosis except in as far as people are confused into thinking both are the same.[22]

In a text written for intending stage hypnotists, Nelson instructs them that

> experience has shown down through the years that the hypnotic show must be faked, at least partially so, to hold audience interest and be successful as entertainment . . . The successful hypnotic entertainer of today is actually not interested whether or not the subjects are really hypnotized – his basic function is to entertain. He is interested in his ability to con his subjects into a pseudo-performance that appears as hypnotism.[23]

We are all aware that phenomena similar to those in stage hypnosis also occur naturally when people have their attention distracted. For example, 'She did not feel pain when the needle was inserted because she was distracted', or 'The soldier did not notice his leg was broken until later because he was so intent on the battle.' Since such surprising inattention can occur without hypnosis, we rightly question whether clinical pain management using hypnosis may be explained in other ways.

This whole question of the reality of hypnosis is important enough to have generated a good deal of research in recent years. Experimental subjects have been instructed to behave as if they were in hypnosis, and the extent to which they can reproduce the same effects as those who are formally in a trance state is remarkable. These studies have involved 'simulators', people instructed to mimic hypnotic behaviour without actually being in hypnosis. This work has led to a better understanding of what happens when suggestions are made, but professionals remain divided as to whether a separate state exists. Some argue that it does not. Many favour retaining the concept of a hypnotic state, and identify features which do stand out. Andre Weitzenhoffer is one who argues that a distinct hypnotic state can be generated and has argued that four suggestion effects provide the basis for referring to a state of hypnosis.[24] Briefly, he refers to these as hyper-suggestibility (going beyond the person who is ordinarily lightly suggestible, and showing that in trance this tendency is enhanced); spontaneous amnesia (forgetting after a trance

---

[22] Barber, T. X. (1986), 'Realities of stage hypnosis', in Zilbergeld *et al*, op. cit. ch. 4.

[23] Nelson, R. A. (1965), complete course in stage hypnotism, quoted by Barber in Zilbergeld, Edelstein & Aaroz, *Hypnosis* p. 22.

[24] Weitzenhoffer, A. M. (1989), *The Practice of hypnotism* (2 vols.), (New York: Wiley).

what was happening even without any instruction to do so); literalness (taking words to have very concrete meanings rather than as abstracts); and different logic (thinking in less orderly ways in favour of loose associations of ideas), often referred to as trance logic.

For the Christian, the question of stage hypnosis is best resolved by saying 'Avoid it.' The use of this powerful experience for such exploitation should not be encouraged. If there are dangers in the skilled clinical use of hypnosis, where an atmosphere of trust has been developed, and ongoing contact maintained, it should be clear that the stage situation can put people into a situation of vulnerability. It is possible for a hypnotist to make a suggestion that is dramatic and safe on many occasions, but for it to have special meaning for an individual that could never have been anticipated. The results can be traumatic. To minimize such risks, a number of attempts have been made to curb stage hypnosis by legislation. Though desirable in intention, they have met with little success as they are so difficult to enforce. They rely on hypnosis being defined in a legally satisfactory manner. The assortment of definitions that exist shows how problematic this can be.

There is no such thing!

It should be clear from the comments on stage hypnosis that a great deal of what is often attributed to hypnosis can actually occur without it, so the question arises whether there is anything uniquely associated with hypnosis. If not, then the term is better abandoned. Indeed, in view of the apparent power and danger of hypnosis, it is ironic that there is a body of opinion which challenges whether hypnosis actually exists at all. This challenge does not dismiss the phenomena as unreal. Rather it says that, while the phenomena exist, they cannot be attributed to a state clearly different from other states including normal consciousness.

Challenges to the reality of hypnosis come from failing to identify the hypnotic experience sufficiently clearly. Since there are other similar states which are also associated with changed behaviour (e.g. drug induced states, focused attention while studying) it becomes rather easy to discuss observed changes as nothing but something else. While this particular view on hypnosis is of great scientific interest and the subject of professional debate, it will not be pursued here. The starting point for this discussion has been that hypnosis does exist as one form of ASC. If hypnosis does *not* exist, there is really nothing for Christians to be concerned about, and clinical work supposedly using hypnosis must attribute its results to something else. On the other hand, if we assume that there is an identifiable state of hypnosis, this leads us to ask about its practical usefulness in the healing process.

Summary

The exploration of what hypnosis is and what it is not has involved a consideration of the scientific definitions, predominantly directed to clinical hypnosis used in hypnotherapy. While some Christians continue to express reservations, there are also competent practitioners who argue for the use of hypnosis by Christian people. They suggest that the rejection of hypnosis is based on false information.

The area of stage hypnosis is one which, while having something in common with the other uses, relies heavily on illusion and showmanship. The elements of dramatic entertainment and pseudo-hypnosis mean that many people, for whom this is their first contact with hypnosis, gain a false impression of its clinical validity.

Because the boundaries of hypnosis are so uncertain, and the possibilities of simulation are so great, some people question whether there is a distinct entity called hypnosis. The conclusion drawn here is that there is such a state, characterized by features of suggestibility, amnesia (sometimes), and changed thought processes.

Chapter 3

Help through Hypnosis

Before considering help

In spite of, or perhaps because of, its long history, hypnosis is still often looked at askance when its therapeutic use is suggested. Although there are many trained professionals in medicine, psychology and dentistry equipped to utilize hypnosis, and some of these professionals are using hypnosis most of the time in their work, there are still not many people who consider a hypnotic approach as the first choice for dealing with problems. More often it is a last resort when all else has failed. It is quite remarkable, therefore, that so many highly successful results are to be found, and for so many different conditions.

Those who are considering hypnosis as a possibility should also be aware that it is widely and successfully used for coping with many normal coping situations. The basic approaches of hypnosis have been developed to assist top sporting personalities and teams in such areas as football, golf and tennis. Olympic teams frequently travel with a psychologist as part of the training support staff, and hypnosis can be an effective part of that person's interventions. The benefits of enhanced attention and access to memory have encouraged its use by students studying for exams. Good results appear to arise not only from those elements but also from associated relaxation, further helped by the incorporation of beliefs regarding self-confidence and ability to offset self-doubts. At the time of writing I am the proud grandfather of several grandchildren. As part of their preparation for childbirth, my daughters were taught hypnotic techniques to assist them to deal with all the stages of labour, as well as the post-natal experiences, to provide safe delivery and positive bonding with their babies. The outcome was very positive in each case, with remarkably straightforward and very short labour, and delivery was always within one day of prediction. The mothers were less tired than expected, and more closely involved with their babies right from the start. Pain control has been another bonus since less use of drugs to control pain leaves the mother more able to be consciously involved in welcoming the arrival of the baby.

These three areas illustrate the wide possibilities for using hypnosis in everyday life. However, before selecting this as an approach, there are usually many questions to be answered. Some of these are general and recurrent, and relate to misunderstandings and ideas noted in previous chapters. Others are more specific to the concerns that Christians have about issues such as will, personal choice and influences, as well as the spiritual questions about demonic involvement. These can readily be explored if a Christian is seeking treatment from a therapist who is also a Christian, but the spiritual concerns are not easily explained to, or understood by, secular therapists. Therefore, some general answers here may help those who are uncertain about the wisdom of utilizing hypnosis.[1]

In addition to brief answers to the most commonly raised concerns, we shall go further in later chapters to see how these issues work out in practice from real-life examples. A practitioner may give a self-serving answer to a question, but good outcomes and the accounts of satisfied users are more impressive.

1. Will I remember anything?

The short answer is, 'Yes, if you choose to.' While a few people (typically those who are excellent hypnotic subjects) remark on a loss of memory (amnesia) spontaneously afterwards, most often a therapist will suggest the option, saying something like, 'You may choose to forget some of what has happened, or all of it if you prefer. But you will be able to recall all that you need afterwards, and what you can handle emotionally.' A suggestion of this kind leads to the person making their own selection, so there need be no fear of either too little or too much later recall. I find that, with such an option, people are very perceptive about what they need, and protective against anything that they are not yet ready to deal with. It is also a feature of hypnosis that memories can be made *more* readily accessible (as in remembering past traumatic events) and this so-called hypermnesia can be useful in resolving fears that were previously not understood. However, we can never be quite sure how much of this

---

1 A generally helpful source for this purpose is Zilbergeld, Edelstein & Araoz, *Hypnosis*.

'improved' memory is factually correct and how much has been constructed to help make sense of what is happening.

2. *I do not believe in passing over control of my mind to anyone*

I consider this to be the single most important issue to clarify, and I will raise it with people as a possible concern if it is not brought forward spontaneously. For three reasons it deserves careful attention. Firstly, everyone has fears about being taken over by others or losing control. Secondly, those who come for therapy have often experienced some kind of victimization and a serious loss of control over their own lives. Control is consequently a basic issue in its own right and, if the right understanding is not achieved from the outset, failure can be expected. Thirdly, Christians are especially sensitive about allowing another human being to take control lest this usurp the role God has in their lives.

By way of response, I would first acknowledge that hypnosis can be practised in such a way that one relinquishes control and comes, for all practical purposes, under the influence of another person. In stage hypnosis there is a deliberate effort to use the dimension of suggestibility to take over a person's freedom of choice and align it with the will of the stage hypnotist. A good subject for this purpose is not only suggestible but also highly compliant. An initial voluntary choice is made to participate by going up on stage, but after that there is a good deal of pressure to go along with whatever is suggested. Most often this is not a problem, but the situation can develop in ways unanticipated by all concerned. There was, for example, wide publicity in Britain in September 1993 when a healthy 24-year-old woman participated in stage hypnosis at a public house. At the end of the performance she was told, along with other participants, that she would experience a shock of 10,000 volts, and then become alert. The woman returned home, complained of dizziness, and was found dead in bed the next morning. The possibility of a link to the hypnotic experience cannot be excluded, and the dangers of such a suggestion deserve to be taken seriously. Nonetheless it cannot be certainly concluded that the hypnotic experience was in fact implicated, and the pathologist involved was of the opinion that hypnosis was not involved. A number of alternative explanations for what happened have been provided by Michael Heap.[2]

In response to public concern in Britain over the hazards of stage hypnosis, a Home Office Committee was established and reported its

---

[2] Heap, M. (1995), 'A case of death following stage hypnosis: analysis and implications', *Contemporary Hypnosis*, *12*, 2, 99–110.

findings in 1995. The committee acknowledged that there is a degree of risk, but found little actual evidence of harm. They found, in summary, that 'stage hypnotism presents no serious risk to the public and should not be banned'. They also made some recommendations to local authorities regarding the tightening of procedures to minimize risks even further.[3]

In religious rituals, there is every intention of taking over the participant, or letting oneself be taken over, in order to enter into the spiritual experience that is sought. It would be very difficult to know exactly where a person is making truly informed choices and where this moves over to relinquishing control to another. Adrian van Leen, who has studied sects and the occult, warns Christians about this danger:

'I don't believe that hypnotism is necessarily occult *per se*, but the heart of the problem is that you are allowing someone else to take control of your mind.'[4] This objection is raised more strongly by John and Mark Sandford: 'Hypnosis is strictly forbidden. One reason for this is that we are not to surrender our will to anyone other than Jesus. A second reason is that such surrender opens the inner psychic doors that only the Lord can enter. A third is that no one besides Christ can be trusted to rule our will.'[5]

In clinical hypnosis *an awareness of the dangers of taking control of others has brought a major shift in the way most practitioners proceed. In the exploratory days of Mesmer, in the late eighteenth century, a highly authoritarian approach was adopted, as the hypnotist proceeded with expectations which were then fulfilled by his subjects. The belief that this is still the essence of hypnosis* lives on as direct and controlling methods are still used. The swinging watch, the flashing light, the commanding presence create expectations that control must be relinquished if hypnosis is to proceed.

A potential subject should be cautious of such approaches and preferably seek some alternative treatment since these methods are quite unnecessary. Many present-day practitioners attribute a different approach to the pioneering work of Milton Erickson, who has been the inspiration for a whole movement of non-directive hypnosis.[6] Erickson was not against a directive, authoritarian approach, since he used it very effectively at times. But he has led the way in showing that a more collaborative interaction can be at least as effective.

---

[3] British Psychological Society (1996), 'Stage hypnotism – no serious risk', *The Psychologist*, *9*, 1, 3.

[4] Quoted in *New Day International* (May 1988), 9.

[5] Sandford, J. & M. (1993), *Comprehensive guide to deliverance and inner healing* (Grand Rapids, MI: Baker Book House), p. 329.

[6] Rossi, E. (ed) (1980), *The collected papers of Milton H. Erickson, M. D.* (New York: Irvington).

This non-directive approach, involving conversation rather than formal induction, indirect allusion and metaphor rather than commands, together with agreed goals and purposes, provides a quite different environment from that which traditionally has been feared. It is based on the skilful use of communication at various levels, by words, gestures and metaphors.

I feel comfortable about offering this approach to any who ask, since it can meet all three concerns mentioned above. There need be no fight over who is in control, since control is deliberately left with the person going into trance. The person with specific fears over control issues can be helped to see that, far from losing control, an increase in control can occur as areas of life which were previously chaotic become manageable. This unexpected paradox can produce a significant relief and reassurance. As the following description indicates, hypnosis is not a matter of giving over control of the mind, or relinquishing one's will to another person. 'Hypnosis is an altered state of consciousness produced in the context of a very special interpersonal contract and transaction where one (the subject) gives over to the other (the hypnotist) the atypical trust of directing his/her stream of consciousness.'[7]

This description rightly emphasizes both the initiative of the person who chooses to give over to the other, and that what is given over is not control or will, but the stream of consciousness.

To be fair, it should be said that, while the hypnotist can facilitate the retention of control, this occurs within the framework of the hypnotist needing to maintain safe boundaries for the experience based on professional knowledge of how to proceed safely. That is, there is an over-arching responsibility for the hypnotist to create, without being intrusive, a safe environment which the client has the freedom to explore within limits.

This balance in favour of the client's self-control becomes even more critical for the Christian. In my view it is unethical to engage in a practice which removes freedom of choice from another person. My role is actually to enhance this freedom and to act in support of the principle that the Christian is to be characterized by self-control as an expression of the fruit of the Spirit (Gal. 5:23). Most Christians will acknowledge that they have less control than they wish over some areas of their lives – habits, addictions, fears, sins – and are seeking to enhance control. The person who is overwhelmed by fears (a phobic person) would acknowledge a lack of control in areas of life. The agoraphobic who cannot go shopping, or the flying phobic who dare not board an aircraft, has lost

[7] Walker, W.-L. (1993), 'Hypnosis – the healer within', *Australian Journal of Clinical and Experimental Hypnosis*, *21*, 2, 15–21.

control of a part of life. Effective management of this anxiety results in a return of control so that what was once impossible becomes possible again. The person has learned how to exercise self-control over an area of previous chaos. Hypnosis can be a tool to help those who are seriously motivated to change.

This position is clearly different from the cautions offered by the Sandfords who characterize all hypnosis as manipulative, controlling, and dangerous. This is an unfortunate caricature which may help to keep many Christians away from a significant source of help. It is also an ironic objection when one considers the manipulative abuses of power in the extended sessions of casting out demons, and railing against evil to the point of exhaustion which have too often been seen in the deliverance ministry (and which the Sandfords also acknowledge). Logic surely calls us to argue against such exploitation of human power in both contexts, while preserving a place for respectful interventions in the name of Christ.

One other point about control is worth making. While it is common to find that people are anxious lest they should lose control, it is also possible for the underlying message to be exactly the opposite. Behind the apparent fear 'Are you going to take control of me?' there can also be the wish 'I really want you to take control.' This can happen when there is a magical belief about hypnosis which assumes that the hypnotist can make things happen to the person who is hypnotized. In effect this is saying, 'I can't do it, but I am relying on you to do it.' Wise therapists resist this invitation. It is based on a misunderstanding, since results must flow from choice not manipulation. The person with the problem must accept responsibility for change. The therapist is not all-powerful, merely a collaborator. Christians will be especially sensitive to preserving the balance which sees God, and not the therapist, as the ultimate source of healing.

3. *Are you going to hypnotize me?*

This question is closely linked to the control issue, and expresses the anxiety about being taken over into an unfamiliar experience. The fear is heightened if we recognize that the context of a consultation has its own inherent hazards. The enormity of the risk that could be present can be understood by imagining of a young woman who has been traumatized by serious abuse coming to consult with an unknown authority figure who is male. Her experience has taught her to be cautious of all men. She comes believing this male is able to take over her mind by asking her to lie back in a chair and close her eyes. This scenario is not an environment for safety, or for a good, therapeutic outcome. However, does anyone have to fear vulnerability with a hypnotist who establishes that control always remains with the subject and who creates clear practices to ensure this? No one need fear such vulnerability.

The reader may have noted that in describing the hypnotic experience I have avoided any reference to 'being hypnotized'. It is cumbersome to refer to 'the hypnotic experience' and 'the subject', or 'the client', as I have variously chosen, but this has been done to emphasize an important principle, namely that clinical hypnosis is a state which should be voluntarily entered as an experience, not something imposed by another. I have found it helpful to startle people who are exploring what is involved in hypnosis, by telling them that I have never hypnotized anyone. This is intended to underline that people make their own choices and can decide if, when, and how they experience hypnosis. By offering general direction, but with a great deal of ambiguity and freedom to explore, I find people can create a highly individual and safe experience for themselves, while I remain in the background.

With this approach the appropriate question then changes from 'Are you going to hypnotize me?' to 'Will you help me explore the hypnotic experience (or trance)?' This is a more helpful way of thinking than referring to the experience as ' being hypnotized'. It is parallel to most of the other ASCs discussed earlier where some level of personal choice is involved.

Restraining expectations is also important in establishing a helpful environment for collaboration. A request to 'be hypnotized' implies the expectation of being passive throughout, while the therapist does what is needed. As has been noted earlier, a tendency to passivity is characteristic of the hypnotic state, but that does not exclude an active participation in the communication process, as examples in subsequent chapters will show. This passive-yet-active paradox is therapeutically valuable and it is not difficult for Christians to embrace it when accustomed to the paradoxical relationship with God which allows Paul to say, 'I live, yet not I. It is Christ who lives in me' (Rom. 8). The active work of God combined with the deliberate response of the Christian has a parallel in the hypnotic experience.

4. *What if I do not come out of trance?*

This question is scarcely necessary if issues of control have been resolved adequately in advance, but it deserves to be answered if it is causing anxiety.

The decision about when to terminate a trance can be managed, collaboratively, with the client advised that they can come out of trance at any time they choose. There can be a problem if the client wishes to stay in trance when the therapist wants to terminate the session because time has run out. The problem is then one for the therapist, not the client! Happily, there are various techniques for negotiating a resolution to the problem.

A related question is occasionally raised. 'What if you (the hypnotist) should have a heart attack and die while I am in trance? Would I be stuck?' It should by now be clear that there is really no problem, since the client is able to choose when to return and will become spontaneously alert without any problem if, for any reason, the therapist were unable to continue. It is commonplace, for a variety of reasons, to enable subjects to alert themselves when they choose, as a deliberate step in establishing self-control. This can be easily achieved through a pre-arranged signal, or a counting sequence which leads to the alert state.

This approach can lead to another technique, which is not only convenient for all concerned but also reinforces the truth that it is the person in trance who is in charge of what happens. The hypnotist teaches a self-induction procedure, making it possible for the subject to go in and out of trance without any external intervention. Under those circumstances it is hard to see how there need remain a concern about 'being hypnotized' or losing control, and it certainly removes all fears about not being able to terminate the trance. This introduction to self-hypnosis is clinically valuable, since some clients are able to use the trance state on their own at home to continue the healing process. There are obvious benefits in this method which can achieve results more quickly and less expensively than those achieved by many consultations.

5. What if I have some frightening experiences while in trance, and don't know how to handle them?

It is part of competent preparation for any procedure, including surgical procedures and dentistry, that the professional is prepared to deal with the unexpected and to handle the worst possible outcome, even though this rarely occurs. In some forms of exploratory therapy using hypnosis, it can happen that the client will access thoughts, memories and feelings that are terrifying. Those who work in the inner healing ministry are familiar with such experiences. However, unlike inner healing, where commonly a team of people is involved to provide ample support, and sometimes continuing for hours, most hypnotic therapy is a one-to-one experience and time-limited. There is, therefore, a heavy responsibility on the therapist to ensure that whatever occurs can be managed, without harm to the subject. An important dimension for the client is that the recall of terrifying experiences is very likely to be associated with an earlier age, perhaps even an age before mature language had developed. Since there is in hypnosis a tendency to re-enter that stage and experience what is called revivification, rather than simply to remember it vividly, it is essential that adequate communication is established at the outset.

It often comes as a surprise to clients that they can talk as freely in hypnosis as in ordinary conversation, so that clinical hypnosis is not totally passive and receptive even though that capacity is enhanced. To be able to say, 'I'm scared', or 'I'm remembering something and it feels too much to handle right now', is a helpful communication. These are adult responses. When someone is responding in a more child-like (regressed) way, other forms of communication can be called on. One client who was worried about this asked me, 'How will I let you know what's happening if I can't speak?' I responded, 'I don't know yet, but you will know when you need to, and I'll be alert at that time.' Sure enough, that time came and she engaged in a most expressive mime which communicated everything vividly.

It is usual these days to prepare beforehand what are called 'ideo-motor signals', pre-arranged gestures or movements which can serve as 'yes' and 'no' indicators. These provide a fail-safe form of communication. Interestingly, these are also non-voluntary movements, so that they express the deep unconscious needs of the person, rather than any superficial, consciously chosen decision. This distinction is frequently important if we want to know what someone really wants, and not simply what they say they want. A fuller explanation of this, and an example of how this can work by following a person's deepest desires, is incorporated in the case study, Example 3 in Chapter 4.

6. If I discover disturbing memories from the past, can I be sure they are real?

This question is of great importance not only in the context of an altered state of consciousness but also in the context of inner healing as a spiritual ministry. The short answer has to be 'no'. We cannot be at all sure that emotionally charged memories from the past are historically accurate in every detail (and usually this is what 'real' means here). I cannot even guarantee historical accuracy if I sit down to recall everything that happened to me yesterday! Ask me about things that happened ten years ago and I shall be very vague indeed and, when pressed, fill in the gaps as best I can to make sense of the story. Ask me about the details of an emotionally distressing time in the past and I shall be even more likely to confuse the story. We well know that if we ask several people about their experience of a disaster, they shall give different accounts with varying degrees of historical accuracy.

When someone in a trance is asked, or chooses, to recall a traumatic event from childhood, there are various psychological mechanisms at work that are guaranteed to distort the story. These mechanisms, which go under names like repression and dissociation, are designed to protect us from harm just as bullet-proof vests are intended to protect us from harm in front-line situations. While hypnosis can often achieve remarkable access to previously lost material, there is no guarantee that when it is retrieved it will resemble the original. On the day I wrote this, a television broadcast reported the recovery of a fifty-year-old German submarine from the ocean bed. The reporter held up what had been a bottle of Scotch whisky and said, 'It may be 50 years old, but I don't think anyone would want to drink it.' He shook the bottle to show a swirling mass of sediment inside. Time changes memories. Emotional overlap contaminates memories; secondary elaboration of memories adds to their uncertainty; personal memories are mixed with other experiences, from our reading and viewing, so that we cannot always know which ones are personal and which ones comes from elsewhere; and leading questions can greatly add to the distortions.

Is there, then, any usefulness in exploring such material? Some Christian writers argue that it is a fruitless exercise, since all we need is the intervention of Jesus Christ to make all things new. Dredging up the past is antithetical to the message of the gospel. I cannot agree with that position. Even for the person who is a thoroughly committed Christian, and totally accepted by God in Christ, there remains much of the old nature and a good deal of cleaning up to be done. For the person who is not a Christian, such explorations can be an opportunity to learn just how much of the past needs to be redeemed.

Today, uncovering techniques, including hypnosis, are increasingly being used to retrieve memories of the past, so that allegations of child abuse arising from newly acquired memories are receiving widespread attention.

This upsurge of interest in memories reported by those who present with histories of childhood trauma and abuses has led to a very serious professional debate over a number of years among psychologists, psychiatrists and lawyers, as to whether these recently retrieved memories can be relied on. My own reading of the debate is that most clinicians will maintain that these memories do represent significant emotional experiences, but they are too uncertain in their detail to stand alone as legal evidence. A significant part of this debate relates to the recovery of memories while under hypnosis, so there are at least two dimensions to the questions. First, can we rely on memories of early childhood retrieved many years later? Second, are memories of this kind retrieved under hypnotic influence more credible or less credible than those obtained in other ways?

The topic is too extensive to address here, but some key points and summary findings from the professions have been included in Appendix 1. The topic is still a relatively new one, having received prominence only over the last ten years or so. Research is therefore still limited, and opinions vary, but the issue is of great practical significance for those who believe they have been abused, and for those alleged to be abusers, since objective claims of abuse obtained by regression techniques are rarely validated independently. Occasionally, independent documentation can be brought forward to provide historical support and at that point such memories may have historic validity. But even that will not validate all the material that a person recalls. Names, places, dates, etc. can be completely wrong because that is the way with memory of all kinds.

So what is the point of such recall? There can still be value in enabling a person to access that which has been long hidden. That it has remained hidden may be an indication that, at the time, it was too hard to deal with. Coming at it again with years of maturity, distance from the original events, and professional support, is a productive way of resolving the stored pain of years. That these facts are not accurate matters little, clinically, provided no allegations against others are based on this material. What is important is getting in touch again with the emotions of the initial traumas, and resolving them. Hypnosis is remarkably well-suited to the task as it enables vivid recall, intense experience of emotion, and an opportunity to reconstruct the past with the use of guided imagery.

The important principle in working with so-called repressed memories is that they do represent reality in a way, but this is not the same as saying that they are historically reliable. It is the stored emotions which matter, more than any particular event. These have to be expressed in some way, and stories of the past provide one vehicle. (Psychosomatic disorders are often another way people represent their emotionality.)

One way to consider this area is to ask, 'When I recall a nightmare should I assume that what I remember really happened?' It is not difficult to agree that many nightmares occur as a way of dealing with disturbing experiences. They can be vivid and emotionally powerful. They are linked to real events, but are not historically accurate. They may represent reality, and skilful interpretation can help to unravel their significance. Nonetheless, when we awaken we say thankfully, 'It was only a dream.' Hypnotic memories are best considered with a similar degree of caution.

The emergence of the False Memory Syndrome Foundation in 1992, based in Philadelphia, has provided a powerful call to be very cautious about assuming objective truth in memories recalled during therapy, with hypnotic recall being particularly vulnerable to the artifacts noted above.[8] While patients often have an intense conviction about the reality of what they recall – graphic stories of victimization and abuse – there are some who have later recanted, blaming this recall on the therapists who worked with them.

These are serious concerns about the extent to which we can believe our own memories of past events, and they suggest that the uncovering approach of hypnosis can have great potential for both benefit and harm. It is not always easy to know which is which, when unconscious material is being explored. From what we know of the non-logical thought processes of hypnosis and of the tendency to visualization of the brain's right hemisphere we can infer that these characteristics shape the recall of emotionally significant experiences. Hence we should expect such recall to be representational, rather than expressions of logical truth.

The emergence of the False Memory Syndrome and its advocates has produced a polarization which places its advocates (claiming memories as false) in confrontation with those who maintain the truth of memories. Under such circumstances advocates on both sides will rally evidence to support their own position, and negate their opponents as fully as possible. My own view is that we would be better served by referring to a Confused Memory Syndrome, where historical events are blurred indistinguishably with fantasy, imagination, and errors of recall which arise readily for anyone trying to remember what happened long ago, especially emotionally significant happenings.

7. *But I've heard hypnosis is occultic, and dangerous for Christians. Is that true?*

This is a widely held view which derives largely from several writers who warned about occultic dangers over twenty years ago. Their opinions

---

[8] For a popular treatment of this, see the cover story of *Time*, 29 November 1993.

have been quoted in many places, and repeated with more or less faithfulness to the originals, achieving credibility through repetition. This concern will be considered in Chapter 8 where it will be seen that the supposed dangers have been greatly exaggerated by drawing from settings in other countries and from other religions where trance-like experiences represent part of spiritual experiences. The fear is raised, by analogy, that practitioners can be deliberately or inadvertently channels for evil when they attend to those who come for hypnotherapy.

Undoubtedly the possibility exists for a therapist to be in touch with evil, and for that person's influence to affect someone who comes for help. A Christian client may be attuned to this and prefer to go elsewhere for help. Also, we know from the mechanisms of suggestion and demand characteristics in trance states that the transmission of ideas and values is more readily achieved in trance than at other times. Hence, for those conditions where change may involve central life values there is wisdom in searching out a Christian practitioner if possible. It is generally known that therapy is more effective when therapist and client share the same value system, and many Christians prefer a Christian therapist to ensure their own value system is respected.[9]

This consideration is especially important in hypnosis where issues of vulnerability and control are more sharply focused. Whereas, in order to have medicine prescribed, it is not particularly important to find a Christian physician – at this point a competent doctor is what is needed – if the basis for problems includes a spiritual dimension, then it is helpful to enjoy shared values, whatever the therapeutic method. Competence is, of course, also a priority requirement when seeking out Christian therapists: it cannot be assumed. Finding a Christian therapist is less important in the context of hypnosis if the presenting problem is one of pain management, or control of burns, where Christian values may never be directly addressed. Yet there are many contexts where implicit values do influence the way therapy is conducted, and where non-Christian values may hinder progress for the Christian.

The central question will really revolve around the issues 'What is the source of healing?' and 'What is the purpose of healing?' The Christian will usually believe that ultimately God is at work, in love, to bring about healing. A hypnotherapist who shares this view will use techniques that incorporate that belief, and may use meditation on Scripture, imagery, and the encouragement of prayer. A secular therapist will not incorporate

[9] For a general comment on finding the right kind of therapist, see Hart, A. D. & Hogan, T. F. (1995), *How to find help you need* (Grand Rapids, MI: Zondervan).

these elements and will be more likely to attribute good results to the power of the hypnotic state itself.

A hypnotherapist with another spiritual background (another religion, New Age, etc.) may bring values and beliefs to the situation which, even if not expressed overtly, are at odds with Christian beliefs. The Christian does well to recognize that a clash of values can occur, but their freedom to choose and challenge remains.

The point here is that while the use of hypnosis *may* be associated with dangers of undue influence, this is not the same as saying that hypnosis is intrinsically and inevitably occultic in origin. If that were the case, then there could be no truly Christian hypnotherapists, and any who claimed to be so would be deceivers. The evidence for this can be sought by asking whether Christians subjected to hypnosis are invariably affected badly, with damage to their spiritual life. Even a single example of a Christian being helped, and enriched spiritually, would serve to dismiss the idea that hypnosis is intrinsically linked to evil.

The warning that hypnosis is tainted with the occult is sometimes supported by an argument based on analogy (never a sufficient argument alone, but useful along with others). It is then argued that because hypnosis is used in religious rituals among other religions, we should avoid it, lest we become corrupted by being open to the demonic. If we follow this argument, we should also analyse what else occurs in such religious ceremonies. In order to bring about heightened religious experience and altered states of consciousness, rituals often include a good deal of rhythmic music, singing and dancing, as well as many prayers to the spirits. Are we then to avoid prayer, lest it also open us up to the demonic? Are we to avoid singing hymns, lest the melodies and rhythms take over and lead us into the clutch of demonic powers?

This analogy enables us to sort out the essential from the incidental elements of religious practices. Prayer in itself is not wrong, but the one to whom we pray is what matters. Singing praise is not intrinsically wrong, but to whom do we sing the praise? So too, trance experiences are not of themselves wrong, but the real question is what we do with them. It would be equally easy to dismiss some of the claims of Christian healing groups for being remarkably similar to the phenomena in primitive cultures and associated with other religions. Many of the healing claims also fail to recognize the possibility of alternative explanations, and are in danger of fostering naive superstition. Yet people are blessed, and God is often glorified. We are unwise to dismiss that which we do not understand.

Returning, then, to the questions 'What is the source and what is the purpose of healing?', we can say that the hypnotic state can provide a powerful environment for change, but hypnosis is not itself therapeutic. We can make the choices to pursue change which is consistent with Christian values and goals, just as others can use the trance state for pursuing quite different goals. If the questions raised here are answered adequately to the satisfaction of the one seeking help via hypnosis, there is a good basis for mutual trust and a recognition that, while powerful, hypnosis need not be feared.

8. Are there not other risks of harm from hypnosis?

It is good for anyone seeking help from a therapist to enquire not only about the likelihood of a good outcome, but also about what the risks may be. Medical practitioners routinely caution their patients about known side effects from drugs, and surgeons assess the probable benefits against the risks. The mental health profession is becoming increasingly aware of the need to show what methods work and under what conditions, as well as to look at possible negative consequences. Christian practitioners are similarly researching the same issues together with the relevance of personal faith in the recovery process with very encouraging results.

For hypnosis the key question is a little different, because it is not hypnosis itself which brings benefit (or harm) but rather the therapy process for which hypnosis is merely the vehicle. Hypnosis is merely one way in which therapy can be delivered. The parallel is not so much with surgery but with the scalpel being used for surgery. Concerning hypnosis, the equivalent question is not, 'Is surgery effective for appendicitis?' but 'Is the scalpel sharp? Is it in good hands? Has it been well sterilized?' We need positive answers to those questions before we can predict the outcome of surgery. With hypnosis, the possibility of harm comes from its incompetent use, from under-trained practitioners and unethical practices. It is to protect the public from such hazards that the major professional bodies associated with hypnosis provide training which is examined, act on complaints of unethical practice, and limit practice to those professionals which already have their own ethical code of conduct to guide them. Medical practitioners, psychologists and dentists are the three classes of professionals most widely embraced by professional hypnosis societies as they have prior professional training and ethical codes. The potential consumer should always be cautious about working with a lay hypnotherapist, since the professional guarantees do not apply.

Where a practitioner is not linked to a profession, and is not a member of a hypnosis society, it is a case of *caveat emptor.* It is wise for the Christian to ask someone who offers hypnotherapy about their training, their experience, and their world view. Given the necessity of a very high level of trust in the professional's integrity, and the vulnerability that can exist when sensitive and personal issues are explored, it is worth seeking out a recommendation or two from the therapist's colleagues or former clients, if possible.

Complaints and bad experiences do occur from time to time with hypnosis: it is a very powerful technique and carries corresponding risks. In Britain, such dangers have been tracked by Heap and Gibson,[10] who identify individual instances of harm. Most complaints are associated with some form of sexual seduction or coercion, with women being victimized by male therapists. Some of these are attributable to lay therapists. Nonetheless, the profession does takes the possibility of harmful effects seriously. Following the survey among Australian practitioners by Judd, Burrows and Dennerstein in 1985,[11] the British Society of Experimental and Clinical Hypnosis also surveyed its membership. West, Fellows and Easton found, on the basis of 148 returned questionnaires, that 32 per cent of the respondents had experienced unexpected complications in their work, and concede that whilst complications are not frequent, they are by no means uncommon.[12] In professionally competent hands, the hazards of any kind are very low indeed, and generally get reported on a case-by-case basis because they are so few.[13] In view of the widespread use of clinical hypnosis and its power to bring about profound changes, the level of reported harm is actually surprisingly low. It will remain so, if consumers take note of the recommendations above.

On the other hand, the benefits may range far more widely than might have been anticipated. Typically, people seek help for a particular form of behaviour, like a fear of flying or an addiction to smoking. Hypnotherapy, to achieve a lasting result, may address the more general issue of

---

[10] Heap, M. (1984), 'Four victims', *British Journal of Experimental and Clinical Hypnosis*, *2*, 60–62; Heap, M. (1995), 'Another case of indecent assault by a lay hypnotherapist', *Contemporary Hypnosis*, *12*, 2, 92–8. Gibson, H. (1992), 'A recent British case of a man charged with rape and other sexual offences', *Contemporary Hypnosis*, *9*, 3, 139–48.

[11] Judd, F. K., Burrows, G. D., & Dennerstein, L. (1985), 'The dangers of hypnosis: A review', *Australian Journal of Clinical and Experimental Hypnosis*, *13*, 1, 1–15.

[12] West, V., Fellows, B. & Eaton, S. (1995), 'The British Society of Experimental and Clinical Hypnosis: a national survey', *Contemporary Hypnosis*, *12*, 2, 137–42.

[13] Judd, Burrows & Dennerstein, 'The dangers of hypnosis'.

fear, or the underlying reasons for the addiction, and in doing so bring out positive changes in related areas of life.

9. But is hypnosis not part of New Age teaching?

This concern is not one I would pass by lightly, since it is absolutely true. The New Age movement has embraced many practices which are not new at all in seeking ways to achievement self-fulfilment and harmony. Vizualisation, imagery and hypnosis (especially self-hypnosis) figure largely in efforts to bring about personal change and development.[14] Does this, however, provide a reason for the Christian therapist to omit hypnosis or for the person with a problem to avoid it? Maybe, but maybe not. On the negative side, I know of therapists coming from a strong Christian faith who have found the use of hypnosis beguilingly attractive, and have resorted to strategies which rest on New Age rather than Christian assumptions. Looking for a guiding light within oneself, and looking for the wise guru who will know what to do, are at best sub-Christian approaches. Those who believe in reincarnation often search for and believe in manifestations of previous lives, even though such accounts can be as easily discredited as the pseudo-memories generated by therapists asking leading questions. The drama and unusual accounts offered by people in trance are seductive to a therapist who can easily lose sight of the paradigm shift which occurs when we abandon biblical teaching about humankind. It is tempting to take these phenomena as somehow 'proving' the reality of what is described.

There is now a good deal of professional literature available about hypnosis written from a New Age perspective, and many secular therapists without theological understanding incline to the propositions as truth. Such acceptance should not surprise us if New Age theologizing is the major source of information about those inner realities we call spiritual. If Christians back away and simply vacate the field, then these interpretations will become the common wisdom about spirituality. If Christians refuse to touch hypnosis, lest it should be tainted with New Age philosophy, then they generate a self-fulfilling prophecy since there will be no other informed voices heard, only the strident cries of Christian sideline critics who have never been involved with what they reject. The danger is there – it is real, and probably growing. Just as a good many of the pressing problems of society grow as Christians fail to participate, so

---

[14] Kelly, A. A. (1990), 'Hypnosis and self-hypnosis' in Melton, J. G., Clark, J., & Kelly, A. A., (eds), *New Age Encyclopedia*, (Detroit, MI: Gale Research).

the probability that the practice of hypnosis will become sub-Christian or anti-Christian will increase if we refuse to take it seriously.

On the positive side it must be said that the New Age movement did not invent hypnosis. It has merely recognized as something ancient, tried and true, and powerful, and adapted to suit their particular philosophy. It is equally true to say that over many centuries Buddhists and Hindus, and Native Americans, and many other religious groups have recognized the power of altered states of consciousness and harnessed them to their respective needs. Christian practices do not have to be exclusively Christian to be valid. If they did, we would never pray, chant, sing, dance or worship – because these are all to be found in other religions. Again the key question is for what purpose, or goal, we do them.

A hypnotic technique that seeks to access some inner helper without acknowledging the Holy Spirit is missing something. A trance that assumes that all we need can be found in our own resources, without need of God, is deficient for Christians. A focus inward without a focus upward is missing a dimension. There are differences for the Christian, yet we must also acknowledge that the differences are not vast; other spiritual traditions are seeking similar ends in similar ways. We do well to exercise discernment in recognizing that which brings us closer to God and that which seeks provide an attractive substitute.

As for me, I am no more dismayed that hypnosis is utilized by New Age practitioners than I am at their delight in using the rainbow as a symbol. We do not need to shun the rainbow because New Age people use it widely. The rainbow continues to represent my hope in a God who knows how to deal with sin, and hypnosis is a vehicle I have been given to help those in need find healing.

Beyond these personal benefits for those in need, there is also a positive need to reclaim this boundary area of psychological and spiritual experience if we can demonstrate that Christians can have experiences through hypnosis which strengthen their faith. If the experience of powerful imagery in trance can enhance a sense of the very presence of God; if powerful healing can occur in the context of the loving and close presence of the Comforter; if prayerfulness can be enriched and deepened, then it is time we said so, and encouraged Christians to enjoy the riches of such benefits, without having to rename their ASC as meditative prayer or inner healing in order to retain credibility. These other terms are not synonymous with hypnosis, but there is a good deal of overlapping experience.

If such a proposal appears shocking or radical, we can gain courage by observing the use of the word 'trance' (or *ekstasis*) in the New Testament. Whereas the critics of hypnosis have substantiated their claim by reference to 'charmers' in Deuteronomy, the text of Acts is much more relevant. The term 'trance' is used in Acts 10:11, 11:5 and 22:17 to refer to a person being out of himself, in an absorbed and receptive state. Luke 10 describes Peter's experience of going to the housetop to pray and falling into a trance. Peter retells the story in Acts 11, and reaffirms that it was as he was praying that he entered a trance and saw a vision. This event is one of the watershed moments of the church, since it led to great preaching in the power of the Holy Spirit, and the spread of the gospel to the Gentiles. Equally positive is Paul's experience recorded in Acts 22:17, and the events are similar: 'when I . . . was praying in the temple, I fell into a trance and saw him [Jesus] saying to me make haste'. The instruction to Paul was also linked with taking the gospel the Gentiles (Acts 22:21). It is difficult to see that trance states can be inherently evil when they are linked so powerfully to prayer, visions (the Lord being involved on both occasions) and commissioning to preach. It is easy to see a natural link between the prayerful attitude and an openness to a special focused experience of God that inspired these two men to proclaim the good news through words.

While a good deal of healing occurs at the level of feelings, with little access to adequate words to describe them, hypnosis places a very strong emphasis on the significance of words, considering them to be powerful symbols for mediating healing. At this point it intersects with the gospel which teaches us not only that words are powerful, but also that the Word, as the incarnation, is the ultimate source of our healing since the Word was with God and the Word was God. This point is well made by Shirley Sanders, who, in reviewing the religious dimensions of hypnosis, comments:

> The New Testament also has citations emphasising the power of words to affect us . . . the power of words in religion provides a channel for man to gain control of his life and understanding from God. The Word expresses God's power to act. Words are used in prayer to thank God, to ask for God's help, or to seek quiet acceptance. Words of prayer renew hope and courage. They offer a model of behaviour to be initiated. They are powerful indeed.[15]

Her point is that not only are words powerful, but they are more powerful in their impact on those in a hypnotic trance state. Consequently, it is very important that words are used with great care. In particular, since

---

[15] Sanders, S. (1991), *Clinical self-hypnosis: The power of words and images* (New York: Guilford Press).

those who seek healing do not always know how that will actually work out, there may be words that have special significance for them and have a profound impact when spoken. It is common to present a symptom, which is then the introduction to many and deeper issues. Sometimes these issues will include spiritual needs. A careful choice to select words that are healing, while avoiding words that might have double meanings, can ensure that the experience is not sabotaged. Sometimes a particular word can have a specially rich significance for a person, and utilizing this fact can speed the process of recovery.

As a therapist, I do not always know what direction healing will take; I certainly cannot force anything through the use of hypnosis. At times it can be a pleasant surprise to discover what has happened while I was attending to other things. This was the case with someone I treated for two years. She initially came with many symptoms of extreme anxiety and insisted we deal only with those, through there were other issues she did not wish to address. Only after some months did she allow me close enough in to her extensive trauma to find that she was a well-defended multiple personality. For the next 18 months I worked with her in efforts to achieve reintegration of her dissociated parts, with some success. Along the way she expressed the wish to have the demons in her cast out. I took this request seriously but, as we worked, it became clear that this was her way of seeking relief from the inner turmoil of conflicting emotions and impulses, rather than a call for exorcism.

About a year later she sent me an unsolicited letter by way of thanks for her progress. I was interested that she made no mention of resolution of her separated parts, but described instead some aspects of life which had resolved as we had worked, and to which I had devoted only limited attention. Among the 20 identified benefits, she listed:

- nightmares not as frequent
- sleep problems not so great
- I clean up my house for visitors, but not so as to overcome my sense of dirtiness
- take no asthma medication
- don't have the strong sense of being contaminated, so I find it easier to hug friends
- gaining in my self-awareness and seeing meaning in things I never understood
- headaches now rare

She also commented: 'Now I see that the fear I had developed of my reaction to hypnosis was the closeness I was getting to painful memories. After success with migraine treatment at age 20 [with hypnosis] I had sought hypnosis for smoking and insomnia but was left distressed, depressed and frightened.' Clearly, the observation indicates that earlier hypnosis for smoking had been directed only at symptoms, failing to address the deeper issues needing to be resolved. During the two-year period with me her smoking reduced dramatically without any specific therapy seeking to achieve this.

What kind of help?

If we can assume from the foregoing discussion that seeking hypnotherapeutic help is a legitimate activity, then we need to ask, 'What situations may respond to the use of hypnosis?' To answer this we must first underline that hypnosis is not a treatment in its own right – it is a state within which treatments can be effective. If I want to travel from New York to Los Angeles, I can think of various ways of achieving this. In the early settler days, riding on horseback, or in a covered wagon might have been the obvious choices, with walking a very poor alternative. As time passed the train and the automobile became viable alternatives. Gradually small planes moved in, but for most people they were no competition to the buses and coaches. However, the arrival of the modern jet transformed the possibilities so that these days a flight becomes the most common choice. If the early settlers had caught sight of a 747 passing over, they would have looked in awe and disbelief, probably invoking a supernatural explanation and calling it miraculous.

The parallel is not intended to suggest that the jet represents hypnosis, faster and better and safer than all its predecessors (though that comparison is attractive). Rather, I suggest that improvements in therapeutic techniques have been significant this century, and the common denominators of effective therapy – relationship, expectancy, suggestion, etc. – mean that for any particular problem we can expect various kinds of therapy to work. The choice is not which therapy will work, but which of a range of therapies is found to be most effective.

The effectiveness of hypnosis can be compared to the fuel used for my journey to Los Angeles. My journey may be by car, bus or plane, but each is enhanced by good fuel. The therapeutic journey may have one of many names – analytic, dynamic, behavioural, biofeedback, etc. – but when hypnotic techniques are included the journey may be smoother and faster.

To the question 'What kind of help?' there is therefore a surprisingly wide range of answers. When hypnosis is used together with one of the standard therapies, there is promise of even better results than when they are used alone. The breadth of possibilities includes not only everyday coping issues (stress management, exam nerves, etc.), but many forms of emotional difficulties, a wide range of physical disorders, as well as, at the other end of the coping scale, enhancement of functioning beyond the usual, such as improvement in sporting performance. Hypnosis is the fuel of the system. One of the predominant features of hypnosis is its use to achieve relaxation, both mentally and physically. Hence, if we are encountering a problem in which anxiety plays a part, then there is a chance that hypnosis will assist in achieving some benefit.

While the depth psychology approaches have been directed to finding the underlying causes of anxiety, hoping to resolve them as insight is gained, the behavioural approaches, including biofeedback, have addressed the present expressions of anxiety, looking for changes in behaviour and beliefs which can bring control over the anxiety. Systematic desensitization is a well-known example of an approach that searches for that which triggers anxiety or fear, and trains people to respond with less and less fear. Whether it is the trauma of early childhood, victimization as an adult, or current distress such as fear of flying, spiders, etc. the management of these negative emotions to gain or regain control over them is a central part of effective therapy. Hypnosis can play a significant part in achieving good results.

Similarly, with predominantly physical disorders an emotional component is often present, whether as cause or as result. Breathing problems such as asthma, skin conditions such as psoriasis, and chronic anti-immune disorders such as arthritis will usually include a major affective component. Whether a child is very anxious and breathes with difficulty as a result, or, conversely, has asthma and therefore becomes anxious about breathing, is an important diagnostic question. Either way, however, management of that anxiety, and a resulting sense of self-efficacy – 'I can cope: I don't have to be afraid of it' – will bring benefits.

There is a range of disorders characterized by abnormal autonomic nervous system activity (the automatic regulatory system which keeps our bodies in balance without thinking consciously) which can be helped by learning to control these functions through biofeedback (blood pressure, blushing, and chronically cold hands are examples). Some people also find that they can get similar benefits from the relaxation that comes from meditation or hypnosis. A combination of these approaches, together, improves the chances of learning control and maintaining it.

The range of possibilities for changing behaviour and attitudes is almost limitless, governed in part by the innovative creativity of the therapist and client in finding ways to achieve desired goals. 'Almost' should be stressed, since hypnotic techniques are not magical and certainly do not provide a panacea as some would wish. Yet they do range more widely than many others suppose. In the critique of hypnosis provided by John and Mark Sandford in their *Comprehensive guide to deliverance and inner healing*,[16] their clear assumption is that hypnosis has to do with the exploration of deeply repressed traumatic experiences, and their concern is that hypnotism (sic) may reveal what the Lord is not yet ready to heal. They do not entertain the possibility that hypnosis might be used with the help of the Holy Spirit, but the case studies reported later in this book indicate that a very comfortable collaboration is possible.

The much broader applications of hypnosis are scarcely considered by the Sandfords, though John Sandford acknowledges his conceptual difficulty in finding a reason why hypnosis should not be used for the control of pain, including dental pain. In the face of a vast literature showing striking therapeutic benefit for sufferers from chronic pain as well as well-documented cases of dental procedures carried through without anaesthetic, Sandford falls back on a proof-text approach to say simply that the word of God forbids it. The proof text once again is the reference in Deuteronomy to snake-charmers. I am not sure whether my dentist colleagues would be offended at such an association, or simply laugh. It is unfortunate when such a myopic view of hypnosis may discourage many from seeking powerful relief from suffering.

As we increasingly recognize the biochemical basis for many forms of depression, it is clear that psychological interventions should not be the first choice for these. Medication is vital and often life-saving. Hypnosis may be a useful adjunct in the background, especially after the most serious elements of depression have lifted and choices are more easily made. Explicitly spiritual interventions are also likely to be more effective when the biochemical balance has been restored.[17]

There is debate about the usefulness of hypnosis with psychotic disorders, such as schizophrenia. Most therapists will agree that the detachment from reality, and the distortions of experiences already occurring among schizophrenics, make hypnosis at best a hazardous intervention. A few courageous (or foolhardy) practitioners believe it can be used, but there is very little clinical support for this at present. By

---

16 Sandford, *Comprehensive guide to deliverance and inner healing*.

17 Tan, S. Y. & Ortberg, J. (1995), *Understanding depression* (Grand Rapids, MI: Baker Books).

contrast, the condition known until recently as multiple personality disorder (MPD), which has often been confused with schizophrenia, is very well-suited to hypnotic therapeutic strategies. Now renamed Dissociative Identity Disorder (or DID),[18] it is characterized by a fragmentation of the personality into many parts. The mechanism of dissociation by which this is achieved, and which serves to protect the person from even more serious disruption, is found to be well-developed in those who are good hypnotic subjects. Some suggest that DID sufferers have used spontaneous hypnosis to achieve many ASCs to deal with various facets of their lives. Since they are so familiar with, and so skilled at using the trance state, it follows that therapy which harnesses this ability might be the best choice of treatment. For less severe conditions, and especially when considering the everyday problems of living (anxiety, stress, sleeplessness, etc.), help can often come through hypnotic techniques in a different way.

Although we usually associate counselling and therapy with help provided by one person to another (or to a group), there are many situations where people can best help themselves once they know how. Hypnosis can play an important part in this, since self-hypnosis has been developed to enable people to learn how to enter and leave a trance safely on their own. Once taught how to do it, and having developed confidence in their ability, many people find self-hypnosis a highly acceptable and very effective way of bringing desired change. If, for example, a person has difficulty getting off to sleep at night, then help is needed that will be effective at a time and place that the hypnotherapist is not available. While there are techniques that can be effectively used elsewhere, it is essential to any approach that it shall work when and where it is needed. Self-hypnosis permits entering a trance state at the time of retiring to bed, and following sleep-related suggestions which can be self-selected to fit the situation. The therapist serves as initial guide on how to proceed, and as a backup if difficulty is encountered, but the action is with the person alone. It is tailor-made, comfortable, non-threatening, inexpensive, and it works!

Similarly, a top tennis player cannot have a hypnotherapist standing alongside them while they are serving, or in the background while they are receiving. That does not preclude carefully planned self-suggestion in a practised trance state. Watch a top-flight pianist or guitarist playing in a solo performance, and ask yourself whether this person is in an altered

---

[18] See the *Diagnostic and statistical manual of mental disorders*, 4th edn (1994) (Washington DC: American Psychiatric Press).

state of consciousness. Better still, ask the performer, and you will find that, either deliberately or quite spontaneously, they can report a shift of awareness within which they can produce a peak performance.[19]

In other words, at times when help is needed but access to a therapist is not possible, the use of hypnosis is still possible. Thus, for the many clergy and pastors who, during the course of their ministry, become anxious and even panicky about standing up in front of the congregation to preach, learning to use effective relaxation and self-hypnosis can be a great assistance in what is very often a stress-related psychological problem, not a spiritual one. In another case I worked with a physician who, after several years in a quiet general practice, developed a fear of blood. By being involved in routine procedures he lost that desensitization which is a necessary part of medical training, and he was afraid that, should he suddenly be called to a major accident, he might faint on the spot. He was an excellent candidate for helping himself and celebrated the end of treatment by going on a two-week refresher course in obstetrics in a major teaching hospital, working in the delivery room without qualms.

Not everyone manages self-hypnosis with ease. Some prefer and perhaps feel safer, to have the therapist's voice close by. Hence, in recent years it has been possible to help people through tape-recorded sessions which they take home and replay as frequently as they need. What does this tell us about hypnosis? Clearly the person in trance is in charge of deciding when and how to use the trance experience. These approaches allow great flexibility in developing help for a very wide range of situations. They can be tailor-made to fit particular needs, and incorporate suggestions chosen by the person concerned. In these days of expensive health care alternatives, they are attractive of the requiring very little of the therapist's time, and maximizing the opportunity for people to look after themselves.

As a final example of this approach to self-management, I recall a middle-aged woman who was referred to me by a Christian colleague. She reported that she had developed a phobia about flying even though for some years she had travelled frequently by air for business purposes. Short trips were distressing, but she was confronting the need to fly from Los Angeles to Europe two weeks later. This allowed her only two visits to analyse the situation and construct an audiotape which she could use prior to flying and then on the journey. She reported later that she was

---

[19] This has been called the 'ideal performing state' by Uneståhl. See Railo, W. S. & Uneståhl, L.-E. V. (1979), 'The Scandinavian practice of sport psychology' in Klavora, M. P., (ed), *Coach, athlete and the sport psychologist* (Champaign, IL: Human Kinetics).

pleasantly surprised at how well she succeeded on the journeys there and back. While I usually prefer longer periods to help people prepare, it is impressive how successfully well-motivated people can find ways to look after themselves once they have discovered the trance state.

Chapter 4

Why turn to Hypnosis

Healing at every level

In the previous chapter we considered some examples of hypnosis in action, assisting people with a variety of psychological concerns, and we noted that there are many physical disorders which may also respond. The effects of relaxation, hypnosis and similar approaches are now widely recognized to be effective with disorders involving the autonomic nervous system and with dysfunctions of the auto-immune system. Similarly, there is an impressive research literature showing that many types of pain can be reduced and made manageable, whether this pain arises from physical trauma, surgery or such chronic disorders as cancer. While some people are able to become completely pain-free, it is usual to teach people to manage their pain in such a way that they are aware of any pain messages which need their attention, in order to ensure that they do not override messages that may need attention in order to get effective medical help. Others are content to reduce the intensity of chronic pain to a less distressing level; or to relocate the pain to a part of the body which is more easily tolerated; or to have periods of time that are pain-free, to allow rest and recuperation instead of enduring unending chronicity.

Some years ago my colleagues and I developed a technique for dealing with tinnitus using these principles.[1] Tinnitus, or ringing in the ears, is a surprisingly common phenomenon, especially as people grow older, yet many of those who seek help are told there is nothing that can be done for it and that they will have to learn to live with it. There is actually a

---

[1] Morgan, C. M., Court, J. H. & Roberts, R. (1982), 'Cognitive restructuring: A technique for the relief of chronic tinnitus', *Australian Journal of Clinical and Experimental Hypnosis*, *10*, 1, 27–33.

variety of treatments available, all of which work for a few people, and none of which work for everyone (probably because tinnitus is the end result of a variety of different conditions). With hypnosis, some people are able to gain control over the maddening sound in their ear as they are taught techniques to change them. We even found people who could transform the sounds into their favourite music!

These examples illustrate some answers to the question, 'Why turn to hypnosis?' The overcoming of fear and reduction of pain are legitimate areas for helping people, and are part of the traditional practice of the health professions. Hypnosis as a part of such procedures is uncontroversial unless we believe there is is something intrinsically wrong in its use.

However, the thinking Christian may want to go one step further and ask whether there is a spiritual dimension to what is done. Since we so easily see spiritual help as the province of the pastor, or chaplain, or priest or maybe the lay Christian counsellor, it is easy to separate out physical and psychological problems as essentially secular and separate from spiritual problems. That is too limited a view of our human condition, in that it fails to recognize the amazing interactions and complexity of problems which can most often be understood only by considering all three areas – the physical, psychological and the spiritual.

Although these interactions are widely acknowledged in hospitals and clinics, there remains a tendency to pigeon-hole people as suffering from one kind of disorder or another. Cancer is generally a physical disease requiring medical attention. Anxiety is a psychological problem for which a psychologist or psychiatrist may be consulted. Doubts about the goodness of God are usually labelled a spiritual problem needing pastoral care. How convenient! How simple! How misleading. In the real world we do not fit into little boxes like that. Increased medical knowledge is making it possible to think of even simple disorders as arising from many factors – predisposition, environment, immediate stresses, family illness patterns, to name a few. Psychological problems are less clearly understood, but multiple explanations and factors are usual. We understand long-standing problems not only by looking back to the causes, but also by looking to the functions served by the condition which maintain them. Spiritual problems are no less complex than psychological ones, albeit perhaps not as fully explored in traditional scientific terms. It is usual to look to aspects like sins of parents, unconfessed sin, backsliding, lack of prayer and other spiritual disciplines, as characteristic of spiritual difficulties.

These three neat categories – physical, psychological and spiritual – are not only painfully inadequate when used in isolation from one another. They also narrow the focus of attention, pre-select the kind of person qualified to help, and anticipate the kind of treatment to be introduced. The implications of this segmented approach can be seen by questioning the goals of those who offer help. For example, what is the goal for the physical treatment of cancer? Typically we look either for a treatment that will cure, or failing that, to contain the progress of the condition. A subsidiary goal may relate to pain management. The choices of chemotherapy, surgery, or other techniques are made by balancing issues of proven effectiveness, available techniques, as well as patient preferences. Yet we might also ask about the psychological goals for therapy, and about the spiritual goals for the person involved. These are not trivial or irrelevant questions, for great benefits can arise when emotional, inter-personal, and faith issues are addressed. A brush with cancer can be an enormously growth-producing experience when all these dimensions are addressed.

What should be our approach to psoriasis, a painful itching condition of the skin? An obvious goal is to restore the skin to normal functioning, and, at first sight, medical intervention appears logical. Yet it is most unusual to find a case of psoriasis without significant psychological involvement. Hence it is recognized to be a psychosomatic disorder. Frequently it is possible to find psychological triggers, emotional events, painful relationships in the background which help to explain the onset and continuation of psychosomatic disorders. Moreover, social and psychological factors can play a major role in perpetuating a condition which might otherwise have resolved. The physical goal of healthy skin will be difficult to obtain with medical treatment alone, or, if achieved, is likely to relapse. When emotional factors are addressed, and relationship issues resolved, the outcome can be much more successful. Good therapy therefore will seek to produce not simply clear skin, but resolution of conflict, both intra-personal and inter-personal.

This still does not take us far enough when we acknowledge the existence of a spiritual dimension to our lives. For the pastor a successful intervention could be a death-bed conversion experience, where the patient dies, but is right with God in doing so. Pastoral work on issues such as shame and guilt, with the healing effects of repentance and forgiveness, is a thoroughly legitimate intervention when spiritual issues are presented. Yet those same issues are often the undercurrent of many other problems which present in physical and psychological ways. No one specialist has all the answers, as the development of multi-disciplinary health teams has recognized: better care is provided as we look at issues from several directions, rather than one.

These reflections on the purpose, or goals, for which we intervene are discursive in order to set hypnotic interventions into a broader context. Because it is very tempting to see hypnosis as a symptom-oriented approach, attending to a specific presenting problem, it is important to realize that such interventions are likely to be very ineffective in the long run. After asking, 'What is the problem?' it is helpful to ask, 'What is the problem behind the problem?' What presents as a physical problem will predictably have other dimensions to it. What presents as a spiritual problem very commonly needs to be seen as having psychological and physical dimensions. Behind a loss of faith, for instance, there is often a depressive illness.

A fully integrated approach to therapy will take account of all these dimensions, with goals appropriate to each. The person who lives with chronic anxiety will, after effective therapy, experience psychological benefit ('I feel more confident', 'I no longer avoid situations,' etc.) But this will go along with physical improvement such as changes in blood pressure, heart rate, and peripheral skin temperature which will improve physical health prospects. Should we not also look for some spiritual gains as these changes occur? ('My life is more joyful,' 'I feel more able to do what God calls me to,' 'I have a greater sense that God loves me.')

Should we not expect that those suffering from the Dissociative Identity Disorder will, in response to treatment, have fewer physical illnesses such as infections and anto-immune disorders, as well as experiencing enhanced psychological adjustment? As the processes of healing advance, should there not also be a sense of God's presence as loving, and of people as supportive? If perfect love casts out all fear, then, as fear reduces, love should return. Spiritual gains should not be a surprise, or incidental, but a significant component of healing at all levels.

Hypnosis, then, needs to be able to embrace such a holistic view of men and women. If the allegation is true that hypnosis is fundamentally evil, or opens people up to demonic influences, then it can only work against recovery. If, on the other hand, the technique is neutral, capable of being used for good or ill, then it is possible to harness this approach to assist those who seek healing at every level – physical, emotional and spiritual.

Practical expressions of purpose

It is a perfectly legitimate activity for a physician to define goals of treatment in terms of recovery from the presenting disease. That is what the professional is trained to do within the medical model of care. It would be quite wrong for the highly skilled physician in a particular specialty to intervene in the multi-dimensional aspects which are outside such training, unless they have also chosen to develop knowledge and skills in those other areas. Hence, most professionals gladly refer their patients to colleagues when they recognize dimensions of a problem they are not equipped to address, and there is a great deal of cross-referral between those trained in the medical sciences and those in the behavioural sciences as each recognizes the skills the other can bring to respond to both physical and emotional disorders.

Purpose for the competent psychologist will commonly mean the management and resolution of emotional and behavioural difficulties. The person with an addiction seeks relief from the addiction and will be content if that outcome is achieved. The marriage counsellor also has a clear set of goals in dealing with marital conflict. The problems may be perceived as existing between two people as much as within any one individual, and resolution is seen in changes in the relationship. The pastor commonly has a different purpose when a member of the congregation seeks counsel. The focus will be not only on the presenting issues but also assumed spiritual dimensions which contribute. A successful outcome will go beyond the presenting difficulties seeking to bring the person into a closer relationship with God and a clearer understanding of God's purposes for them. Each has legitimate purposes defined by the training and conceptual framework within which problems are understood. These are not mutually exclusive. Each can usefully learn from the other and interact in attending to the various ways people may be helped. While there has been a long history of people in trouble making their spiritual advisor the first point of contact (and more recently the family physician is increasingly chosen), this is essentially a gate-keeper role, such that it is always necessary to consider whether the problems deserve the attention of someone else.

If healing does most often involve many aspects of human experience, then ideally members of the helping professions might be trained in all these areas. Since such extensive training is virtually impossible, a good alternative is the multidisciplinary team, bringing together a variety of professionals who know their own area, and respect their colleagues' expertise. This model is increasingly apparent, especially in the area of mental health, with physicians, psychiatrists, psychologists, social workers, marriage counsellors, attorneys and others joining to provide a consortium of skills. Sadly, all too few of these teams include anyone whose primary focus is the spiritual needs of the person. Hospital and industrial chaplaincy are positive examples of how this may work. As such teams have developed, the various professionals have cross-fertilized one another with concepts from quite different training models. A holistic approach by a team means that the patient is no longer an 'appendix', or 'a depressive disorder', or, still worse, a case number, but a person set within a context, whose presenting problems can best be understood in multiple ways.

Within a framework like this it should be clear that hypnosis can take a logical place in the range of interventions, and that it may be used in several quite different ways for different purposes. Most commonly it is employed to assist in therapeutic settings in the management of physical and psychological problems. It is particularly valuable in the interface between these two, that is, the psychosomatic disorders. These are excellent applications for hypnosis whether or not we consider the spiritual dimension. Yet, is there any reason why hypnosis should not also be applicable in those areas where spiritual healing is needed? Not infrequently a person has a physical problem *and* spiritual concerns. Someone, for example, who is facing life-threatening surgery or is suffering a terminal illness needs attention not only to physical concerns but also those ultimate questions about life, death and what lies beyond. Many recognize that they are suffering from an emotional illness, yet realize there are also spiritual dimensions to this. Where abuse has been suffered, there is a need for forgiveness; where abuse has been inflicted, there is a need for repentance; where sinful behaviour brings addiction, there is the need to acknowledge what the recovery movement calls 'the higher power' to bring release. When the problems are relational, as in dysfunctional marriages, there are often spiritual dimensions which need to be addressed – vows broken, spiritual life in tatters, and an absence of living faith in God. Attending to the relationship without these other issues may well produce limited gains because the spiritual is inseparable from the rest.

Within a framework which sees value in healing at all these levels it may come as a surprise to realize that hypnosis can play a part at each level. When hypnosis is seen as a magical intervention which produces instant relief from physical pain, it is tempting to suppose that the intervention is directed purely to the physical discomfort, with improvement a cause for astonishment. When hypnosis is applied to an emotionally based difficulty such as anxiety or fear, and the person reports being free of this, it is tempting to suggest hypnosis is merely symptom-oriented, that deeper issues have been ignored, and relapse (return of the symptom) will occur soon after. When hypnosis is used as a part of unfamiliar religious rituals, as in the development of a frenzy or temporary loss of consciousness, it is tempting to suggest that this is a dangerously occult practice which can only lead people away from a personal relationship with God.

Each of these possibilities is put forward separately to emphasize the danger of thinking in simple categories and apparently simple outcomes. Reality, and the clinical use of hypnosis, is a great deal more sophisticated than that. If we analyse what is happening when something apparently straightforward happens, it proves to be complex. The components of successful hypnosis were outlined above in Chapter 1, and similar mechanisms affect the way other healing techniques work. The power of suggestion and expectation is a common denominator for most successful techniques, even medication, where the placebo effect is known to be powerful.

If we can start from the premise that hypnosis of itself is neither morally good nor bad but a technique to be used, then we can see how it may play a part in healing for physical, psychological and spiritual problems and, more importantly, in those most common situations where all three combine. Then we can identify a valuable purpose in using or experiencing hypnosis as healing in the broadest sense. We can expect good results for a physical disorder when hypnotic techniques focus on influencing physical function. But if there are other issues maintaining the problem, then hypnosis may play a part there too.

Integrative examples of healing

In order to explore how such holistic healing might work to bring relief of presenting symptoms, while at the same time addressing spiritual concerns, the following examples are presented. When the first example[2] was originally published with the gracious permission and assistance of the person described, it was presented to illustrate a point which deserves to be emphasized. As people become aware that hypnosis is not demonic,

---

[2] The following case is adapted from material first published as Court, J. H. (1985), 'A case of congregational healing', *Journal of Psychology and Christianity*, 4, 2. Reprinted by permission.

nor a treatment they have to be afraid of, so those who benefit from it become able and willing to share their experience with others.

While many people who experience therapeutic help are ashamed or embarrassed to let anyone know about it, especially among Christian friends, the following story is one of outstanding courage and integrity. As a result of telling the congregation what had happened, healing spread beyond one person to embrace others who were able to see that they also could reach out for help. Such openness makes it possible for friends to support one another in prayer instead of hiding secretively. That, too, has to be an added benefit since we know that mutual prayer support is powerful – and increasingly there is scientific support demonstrating the truth of this.[3]

Example 1

The case reported here is unusual because part of the healing process involved a public declaration by a pastor's wife to the congregation, for reasons identified below. It illustrates the personal healing of memories in a case of dissociation, using hypnosis for exploration and resolution, together with strong reliance on the spiritual resources of prayer and Scripture. Perhaps most importantly, a willingness to share a personal experience of healing with the family of the local church led to others daring to come forward and seek similar help. Several families have already been profoundly affected.

BACKGROUND

A pastor's wife, Yvonne, aged 36, presented following a distressing period in the local church during which she had been receiving poison-pen letters. They made ugly sexual allegations regarding her unsuitability for her role, in spite of her obviously godly and dedicated life. The congregation shared her distress, praying for her, while the inevitable finger of suspicion moved around, with everyone wondering who would write such indictments.

Exploration using age regression in hypnosis revealed a number of seriously traumatic experiences in her childhood, which were gradually resolved through abreaction, cognitive restructuring and the prayerful involvement of Jesus bringing healing to those events. The major breakthrough came when she became conscious that she was the letter-writer.

[3] Dossey, L. (1996), *Prayer is good medicine: How to reap the benefits of healing prayer* (San Francisco: Harper).

This awareness was followed by deep depression and distress for a period during which antidepressants proved helpful. Her husband had to come to terms with this revelation and did so magnificently. There was an extended period of disturbed dreaming which also provided a focus for therapy.

Gradually she integrated the shadow side of her personality, abandoning her earlier denial and dissociation in favour of acceptance of herself and forgiveness of those responsible for her traumas. Two years after her first therapy session, the eldership of the church agreed to call a meeting of those in the church who had been aware of the earlier letters, so that a full explanation could be offered. An edited transcript follows.

YVONNE SPEAKS FOR HERSELF

> It is exactly two years ago now, that anonymous letters were being addressed me, letters which were clearly expressing considerable criticism of me as a person, and were none too kind in the way they were worded. Receiving letters of that type, with such blatantly expressed accusations, was very hard to take, not only for me, but also for many of you, who, because of your close proximity, were also aware of the contents of some of the letters. I think especially of the folk who were in the choir at the time.
>
> On the last Sunday in August, it was announced from the pulpit, that the flow of letters had ceased, and that the problem was now being dealt with. At that time, no explanation was given. I have no doubt that there were many people who could not help wondering who amongst our congregation, that letter writer could have been . . . I have asked for this meeting to be called so that I could tell you that I was that writer!
>
> I need to say that there never was a time when anything took place from the perspective of a cold and calculating, or premeditated deception. I say that, not to minimize the impact of the revelation, but rather to explain to you that the problem was a deeply psychological one – one of which I was not the least bit aware at the time, and one which, when it finally hit the surface, left me fearing for my very sanity.
>
> I've asked for this meeting to be called, because I've felt very much the need to express my heartfelt regrets to you all, for the suffering – for some of you, quite considerable suffering – that this situation caused. The sense of shock and dismay, even distress, that was expressed – 'How could it be that someone in our congregation could do such a thing?' – was indicative of the heartache felt by many. For those things, I am truly sorry, and I want very humbly to ask for your forgiveness. I have not, until now, been able to be open and honest with folk to the degree that I would have wished. I would really value now the opportunity to share with you something of the incredibly gentle and loving way that the Lord has brought me through those dilemmas to a point where I know a wholeness that never was part of my experience prior to these traumas. I took my wedding

ring off that first mortifying day, because I felt unworthy to wear it, only to be confronted with the Romans 8:28 reference engraved on the inside. Now I had to exercise my faith, and believe that God would be faithful to His word. But how?

Very early in the piece, I read of Paul's imprisonment, and how he believed that he was in that place in order to bring about the greater cause of the gospel. I was in prison too! – A psychological and emotional prison. Could I dare to believe that too could be for the greater cause of the gospel?

As I saw things at that time, everything about my life, my conversion, my ongoing commitment to the Lord, and my involvement in Christian things was all bowled over in one devastating blow, but as became a pattern in months to follow, the Lord gave me encouragement on this day with 'Your words have upheld him who was stumbling, and you have made firm the feeble knees. But now it has come to you, and you are impatient; it touches you, and you are dismayed. Is not your fear of God your confidence, and the integrity of your ways your hope?' (Job 4:3–6). In working through problems, I had to face, in some cases for the very first time, some very traumatic experiences from my childhood and teenage years. Travelling back through some of those horrific memories was very painful, and very hard.

The depression closed in, to a depth that I would never have thought possible. And so began a period where I had to battle with the option of suicide. I was asking the Lord, couldn't He see that enough was enough? His answer came, loudly, clearly, quickly, 'You who seek God, let your heart revive.' Slowly, lovingly, the Lord helped me to pick up the pieces, as He showed me more of His faithfulness to me, and this healing.

It is certain that my life will never be the same again, but I know that I can honestly thank God for what he has taken me through in the last two years. I have a far deeper understanding of the unfailing reality of God's presence, come what may. I can categorically testify that God can and does heal painful memories. No, He doesn't take them away, but because He knows and understands, and because of all that He achieved on the cross, He can remove all the sting. I believe also that through this experience, He has given me a new and deeper understanding and sympathy when others are hurting. Now I know that this experience has been allowed for the greater cause of the gospel.

THERAPIST'S COMMENTARY

I then set the treatment and outcome into context.

Let me first say a little about the unusual aspects of the story and then lead on to the elements to which we can all relate as familiar. First, it is unusual for anyone to do something and to have no conscious awareness of having done it. The separation between conscious and unconscious we call 'dissociation'. It occurs when one part of the personality so strongly disapproves of or rejects what is occurring in another part that there has to be a total denial of the unacceptable part. Some people, like Yvonne, wrestle with internal conflicts which present so great a contrast that sanity is preserved by dissociating what we might call the bad part from the good part. Such a complete dissociation can be easily produced experimentally through hypnosis with certain people. From such experiments we learn how there are different levels of consciousness in all of us, and we can move between them according to circumstances.

It is very unusual for someone who has written what might be called poison-pen letters to be publicly identified, even by accident, let alone by personal choice. It is easier to keep quiet and hope the memories will fade. You have heard why Yvonne chose to take the harder way. From very early in therapy we discussed the need for taking this step eventually – for her own integrity and for the sake of those who might otherwise be inadvertently hurt by what had happened. Healing, to be complete, does require sorting out the tangle, not only within oneself, and before God, but also with those who have in any way been involved. This is a clear biblical principle in relation to sin, and I believe the same to be true in this situation of psychological dysfunction.

I wish to emphasize that among Christians the load of guilt or shame or failure or worthlessness arises very often not from our own misdeeds but through suffering at the hands of others, especially when we are young and relatively helpless or vulnerable. How we deal with those traumas makes all the difference – whether we are destroyed by them or grow through them.

An important verse of encouragement for Yvonne has been that wonderful declaration by Joseph to his brothers. They did so much to harm him, but at the end of the day, in Genesis 50:20 he says, 'As for you, you thought evil against me; but God meant it unto good, to bring to pass as it is this day, in order to bring about this present result.' What a triumphant response!

And so now back to Paul, who in Romans 7, describes the universal dilemma:

> We know that the law is spiritual; but I am carnal, sold under sin. I do not understand my own actions. For I do not do what I want, but I do the very thing I hate. . . . For I do not do the good I want, but the evil I do not want is what I do. So I find it to be a law that when I want to do right, evil lies close at hand. For I delight in the law of God in my inmost self, but I see in my members another law at war with the law of my mind and making me captive to the law of sin which dwells in my members.

Paul is not here writing of unbelievers. He writes of his own Christian experience. He writes of your experience and mine. He describes an ongoing conflict which every Christian faces. Most of us settle for some sort of compromise. Yvonne, however, was faced with a real dilemma. On the one hand, there were traumatic parts of her past experience that she wanted no part of. On the other hand, she had a high view of God's calling. The shadow side of her personality was anathema, yet kept coming back to haunt her. But how could she ever be good enough? One day, surely she would stand accused. And sure enough, the shadow, the traumas of the past, sought to demolish her with accusations of worthlessness and allegations so unthinkable they could not be ignored. She, with the rest of you, was quite properly horrified.

I share with you what I believe to be the turning point in the resolution of her dilemma. It was for me an exquisite moment in working with someone and seeing how the Lord can heal the scars of the past. It encapsulates the integration of professional techniques and God's loving intervention to produce an experience of true healing. Under hypnosis she became able to recall some early events that had distressed her and then said, 'Last Friday I became incredibly angry.' I asked if she could begin to identify the source of the anger, but Yvonne was four steps ahead of me. She said: '(1) that I should suffer such indignity; (2) that there was noone to help; (3) that I couldn't give thanks to God; and (4) I was angry at God for allowing it.' I responded, 'I suppose Jesus could have said that about His sufferings.'

The result was a reframing of her experiences to understand them not simply as her own personal pain but something that Jesus could enter into with her and indeed, by His own suffering, came to heal.

So my final general reflection is this. In most congregations we support one another prayerfully and lovingly if someone suffers a serious physical illness, or breaks a leg, or becomes unemployed, or is bereaved. We rally round, and the support is greatly appreciated. But if one of you has an emotional difficulty, can you share that? Broken legs yes, broken hearts, no. Pregnancy, yes; impotence, no; death, yes; suicidal depression – we'll hush it up as much as possible.

In this congregation you are privileged to have a pastor and his wife able to be honest with you. They dare share their own struggle with you, for your good, realizing they make themselves vulnerable before you. My prayer is that their trust in you is warranted. May their experience of healing enable many of you to know that the Lord is risen – with healing in His wings.

FOLLOW-UP

This public confession was a deeply moving occasion for all concerned, bringing a new sense of fellowship and love to the congregation. Yvonne has been able to undertake extensive training and develop a personal ministry, along with her husband, enabling others to seek help for problems they had never shared before. An effect across families and generations is already apparent.

Example 2

This example represents a similar blending of psychological healing with spiritual growth, in which hypnosis played a vital, though not exclusive, part. The text that follows was given to me some months after we had worked together, with the intention that this one person's journey should be made public for the encouragement of others. It was written by someone who had experienced a good deal of prayer ministry before seeking psychological help. The outcome, in addition to the personal benefits described, was a vibrant return to a pastoral ministry which had been impeded by psychological barriers.

Although I had always hoped, longed and searched for healing of my depression, the possibility of such healing seemed increasingly remote the longer the illness remained and the available avenues of help were tried and found wanting. I had genuinely trusted that God would one day act and I would have a miraculous healing that left me carefree, bubbling and unscarred by my life experiences. Despite the beautiful and valuable ministry of prayer-healing which enabled me to offload much guilt and oppression, the illness remained. Support from a caring G.P. and patient friends kept me from what seemed the only possible escape from an emotional state of unremitting awfulness. I doubt if any depressive has been able adequately to describe his or her feelings at the worst moments, but oblivion was certainly my burning desire at those times.

Yet, since as a Christian I have an intractable belief in God having a purpose for every life and that I have a place in His vast, eternal plan, it was obvious that I could never take the step of suicide, but had to continue my search for the elusive healing. How did it come? Not by an easy, do-it-yourself kit, but through the expert and remarkable ministry of a clinical psychologist with whom God works in a unique and powerful way. As a Christian I had been given to understand that hypnosis was not a good thing, and certainly in the hands of a person without training in psychology or psychiatry and within the Christian context, I would not have entertained such a method of treatment. I don't understand the hypnotic state and am content to leave it that way, but, having experienced it for the purpose of healing, I am convinced that it must have been in God's original plan for some good purpose for such a capacity to be present within us. Step by step, by means of hypnosis, the practitioner took me through the incidents in my life which had stunted me emotionally and had the power to prevent me living my life to the full. Some of the experiences were from my childhood, some as an adult – but all were difficult, painful and preferably to be avoided.

Those for whom Jesus is a living reality in their lives will know, of course, that He was the ultimate healer. Week by week He walked back with me and stood with me as I relived lonely and terrifying episodes in my life. Initially I found it difficult to respond when He took me back to times beyond when I knew Him as a living reality. Although present in my hypnotically produced picture, He was like a figure on one of those felt boards once used in Sunday Schools.

Gradually this changed and, in the final session, I had the wonderful experience of sensing Him picking me up as a small baby out of my cot and giving me the love, warmth and comfort I desperately needed and didn't receive from parents too tired and careworn to respond to the needs of their child. By such an experience, I believe that God was, in fact, altering the history of my life.

Hypnosis was not the only element in my healing. I had a psychologist who cares deeply about the healing of others and whose skill and sensitivity enabled difficult issues to be aired and resolved. And it wasn't achieved quickly. It required weeks of delving into areas I wanted to leave buried – childhood rejection, aloneness, times of terror. It required trust in my psychologist and in what God was doing through him. I had to walk through a wilderness to attain the longed for healing.

Do I still experience depression and other difficulties? Of course I do, because I belong to an imperfect human race, but these difficulties are decreasing with each week and the positives of my experience are emerging. I can tell you that my life now seems worth living. After 13 years of constant sleeping difficulties I now sleep every night; I think clearly, make decisions quickly, and have increased powers of concentration and energy; I find pleasure in doing things that had previously required tedious effort. And, above all, that terrible despair has gone.

Am I carefree, bubbling and unscarred? No, and it was unrealistic to expect such a state. Reliving the horror times involved a grief process with many tears. What I did experience was a spiritual richness amongst the pain and a deeper conviction of the reality of Jesus.

Example 3[4]

A 39-year-old single woman, whom I will call Elaine, recently bereaved by the death of her father and also recently having had a hysterectomy, came to see me with phobic symptoms, a chronic history of arthritis, and severe psoriasis covering most of her body.

Active in her church, she had received great benefit from the pastoral care of an experienced minister who, having moved elsewhere at rather short notice, left her with an unresolved transference. She had been lonely from childhood. Her parents separated when she was five years old, and she was sent to a girls' boarding school. When she was nineteen, her mother died. Throughout her adult life Elaine had struggled over relationships involving men, and eventually reconciled herself sadly to a single life. She relieved the intense loneliness of this single lifestyle by hard work but doubted the quality of her job performance. Throughout this process, extending over about ten years, she had been growing in her faith.

Throughout the many aspects of Elaine's pilgrimage in therapy, the interweaving of hypnosis and private meditation was particularly remarkable, illustrating the complementarity of the two and involving the experience of Jesus as a healer of earlier trauma. This can be seen in her own account which follows.

Elaine's psoriasis had first appeared 24 years previously when she was aged fifteen, and had failed to respond to medical treatments. I postulated that her psoriasis symbolized unresolved conflict in her life as well as providing some kind of solution. She always wore long clothing, which hid the problem since her face and hands were clear.

I proposed hypnosis as a means of exploration and resolution of conflicts, and she accepted this after it was explained that she would remain in control at all times, and that the hypnosis would involve the use of biblical imagery. Because many clients are doubtful and confused

---

[4] Based on material first published in Court, J. H. (1987), 'Hypnosis and inner healing', *Journal of Christian Healing*, 9, 2, 29–35. Reprinted by permission.

regarding hypnosis, and somewhat fearful about the wisdom of Christians' participating in it, I only proceeded after extended explanation of what to expect, and after we had looked together at the objections commonly raised against hypnosis: the risks of demonic influence and of giving over control to another, and teaching that hypnosis is unscriptural. I invite clients to read further, providing them with sources that deal with such issues.[5]

In Elaine's case, treatment of any kind was undertaken reluctantly, as she had received help on other occasions but had always reached a 'block' and could go no further. Regarding early experiences, she said, 'I don't want to open up that again.' But eventually she was receptive to the idea that hypnosis might help in discovering the hidden basis for her psoriasis, and assist in releasing deep inner grief that I postulated had not been expressed in tears.

Using paced deep breathing and careful speaking with eye fixation, I enabled her to reach a state of comfortable relaxation that quickly became light trance wherein a deeply peaceful state is experienced. When employing hypnosis with a Christian, I typically ask my client to visualize their own safe place, describe it to me, and invite Jesus there if they so desire.

A client can vividly and effectively be brought back to significant experiences through hypnosis in a number of ways. He or she may, for example, be asked to walk along a corridor with doors numbered for each year of age. Asked to choose which doors to open, the client is usually able to identify without prompting those doors representing ages when emotionally significant events occurred.

It was quickly evident from the way Elaine talked about her life experiences that she had had difficulty in close relationships, especially with boys while in her teens. It was my working assumption that her psoriasis helped to distance her from male relationships. She also was aware of deep fears of rejection dating at least from the parental conflict when she was about five years old.

While in the trance state described above, she was asked to capture a feeling of rejection, then, using the affect-bridge technique,[6] intensify it, and then to go back to an age when she had experienced rejection

---

[5] e.g. Court, J. H. (1984), 'Hypnosis revisited', *Interchange, 34,* 55–60; Newbold, G. (1983), 'Hypnotherapy and Christian belief', *In the Service of Medicine, 29,* 2, 16–20; Venn, J. (1986), 'Hypnosis for Christians', *Journal of Christian Healing, 8,* 2, 3–6.

[6] Watkins, J. (1971) 'The affect bridge: A hypnoanalytic technique', *International Journal of Clinical and Experimental Hypnosis, 19,* 1, 21–7.

intensely. She located several events, but notably one when she was aged fifteen. To her dismay she found herself looking at a large, impenetrable brick wall. It seemed as though the familiar block had returned.

As we had already agreed that it would help to have Jesus present, I invited her to bring him into the situation, and she did. She became aware of a door in the wall, and I asked if it could be opened. It had a handle and was unlocked, but she reported that as she tried to open it, Jesus seemed to hold it closed. We terminated the session having found a possible way through the block, although clearly the Spirit had indicated that she was not ready to go further at this point.

During the next visit Elaine started by saying, 'I'm feeling very vulnerable.' This time, with the wall again in her mind, besides seeing the door, she also could see over the top of the wall, and there were people on the other side. She described the door as being a dull red, and said, 'I should be able to press lightly and it would open'.

Asked to free-associate to the meaning of the door, she achieved a flood of recognition of a door at school that led to a classroom full of poignant memories: a mixture of sexual awakening and unexpected rejection. She recalled that at this time she had experienced a 'dizzy turn', a feeling that recurred often in the ensuing years.

These recollections, together with memories of the earlier absence of close touching from her father, provided so much painful material that she decided after this session to take a weekend away to work on her experiences privately with God. Her own account, written immediately afterward, best describes what happened.

> In preparing for this special period of meditation it was important for me to, prayerfully, affirm two things; first my belief in God's power to heal and the way in which that had begun to emerge for me. Secondly, that the reconciliation and healing which occurred for us all at the Cross is a timeless act, and one which we can appropriate for ourselves at any stage in our lives.
>
> It has been a joyous journey of discovery for me to work with a Christian psychologist and to find us both being led by the Lord in each session. The words of Scripture given to me were significant to my particular problem – Romans 5:6, 'For when we were still helpless Christ died. By his death we are now put right with God.'
>
> After a short time in which I relaxed and allowed my mind to move from the preoccupations of the day and focus on the Lord's presence, I took those words of Scripture into a scene from early childhood which I still found very painful. It was a scene in which my parents were wrangling about the future of their relationship; I sat there feeling very small, very insignificant and lonely. I was suddenly aware that we were all helpless about our relationships at that time, but

God had acted through the Cross to set it right and I could now appropriate that. If I had any expectations or desires of what was to happen they would have simply involved a reaching out to my father and asking him to hold me, something I could not recall taking place when I was small. Returning to that room with my parents I found myself walking to the door with my mother and asking if she would mind leaving Dad and me alone for a while. She seemed quite happy about this, and as she left, Jesus entered and I held his hand and walked back with him to my father. I was suddenly aware of Dad looking at me with an expression I had never seen before – deep affection, and longing. I stayed with his gaze for a while, just enjoying the experience, the joy of being wanted. I think the tears began to flow at this time and they continued during most of the experience. They were tears of release and joy.

In this manner I became aware that it was possible to talk to my Dad now in a way which had not been possible before. The hurts both of us had experienced had caused many barriers to be erected against an open expression of love and need. Now I felt we had a new opportunity. I told Dad of my love for him, recalled some of the joyous moments of our relationship, and asked him to hold me. He responded positively. At this stage I did not seem able to deeply feel the 'holding', and I believe this will come slowly as the Lord fills in the gaps in my growing up experience.

After a while I sense Dad is turning me towards Jesus whose presence I have been conscious of all along. It seems a very protective presence, a reassurance that this time he will not allow me to be hurt. There is a sense of having to 'let go' at a still deeper level so the Lord can minister in greater freedom. It is important for me to allow these events to unfold, rather than trying to control them.

To my surprise Jesus walks to the door and brings my mother back into the room. There follows a very special time of being held by both parents, of hearing words of approval, of being cherished. For the first time I sense the joy of having loving parents on either side of me. There are many tears on my part.

A short while later I sense they are wishing me to focus on Jesus again. They seem to be asking me to let go of them and of the way we were. At the same time there is a sense that I am to continue enjoying our new relationship. The focusing on Jesus reminds me of the One who is my unfailing relationship and source of security.

I find I am 'farewelling' Mom and Dad. When it comes to Dad I find a deep cry wrenched from me: 'Don't leave me again.' I cling to him, sobbing. There is an immediate sense of reassurance that it is not a permanent 'farewell' but a releasing of the old relationship. With a great deal of adult love I now farewell both parents, telling them what special people they are and how much they have given me in life.

In this time I am conscious that a scene from my childhood seems to cross the bridge into my present adult state, and I relate to my parents as an adult in the latter part of this experience.

I have a 'floating' sense of freedom as I farewell my parents and find myself before Jesus. He lays his hands upon my head and prays for healing of my hurts and fears and for my skin disease. At this time I have a sense of that skin disease floating away from me, though the signs of it are still apparent.

> This is a time of great joy in the Lord's presence, and I realize once more that He is the source of life for me. Gradually I begin to integrate into my day once more.

Subsequently Elaine worked through more deep and painful material. One year from the time she started therapy, there still were issues to resolve. Hypnosis has not always been used, but at strategic stages it has proved valuable in identifying significant events, recalling lost memories, and enabling exploration of painful emotions. I found that dialogue with her in the hypnotized state can also involve conversational prayer and allow her to remain in meditation or praise before terminating the session. Invariably we finished by returning to the pre-arranged place of safety.

I have followed her progress now over several years. She reports that the psoriasis has effectively gone, but tiny patches flare up if she becomes stressed. She takes a warning from this and moderates her life. She has taken a number of significant steps towards more effective coping as the healing process continues. The ongoing resolution has not simply been the healing of her symptoms that are symbolic of her interface with her world; healing of great inner hurts has occurred at deep levels within. She now has an active healing ministry within her own church.

Summary

I have argued that we are complex beings and that it is convenient to think in categories like physical, psychological and spiritual. When we encounter problems, they rarely fall neatly into one of these categories. Complex interactions between the three mean that healing needs to be pursued in all these areas.

While hypnosis is a psychological tool, it can be used effectively for physical and spiritual interventions, and, par excellence, for working in all three areas. The quoted examples, relying heavily on first-person accounts of therapeutic work, illustrate how hypnosis can be used not just to facilitate healing of the presenting problems, but also to produce spiritual growth and enrichment.

Chapter 5

Hypnosis, Religion and Spirituality

In addition to the possibilities for significant healing at all levels which can come from the responsible use of clinical hypnosis, we can go further to consider how altered states of consciousness (ASCs) may impact normal functioning in spiritual contexts. Having noted in Chapter 2 that stage hypnosis is quite different from clinical hypnosis, and that the occultic use of hypnosis is different again, a further step is to look at the legitimate expressions of Christian faith and life in relation to hypnotic phenomena. This further step will be difficult if not downright unacceptable for those Christians who are convinced of the spiritual evils inherent in the use of hypnosis. If that idea has not been adequately challenged in the preceding chapters, then there is little point in reading further, because my intention is to come closer to the personal and sacred experience of our spiritual life.

In choosing the two words 'religion' and 'spirituality' I am not treating them as near synonyms. Rather, I propose to look at two quite distinct aspects of Christian experience. When referring to 'religion', we are identifying that aspect of any faith (Christian, Muslim, Buddhist, etc.) which is concerned with the public expression and collective experience of that particular religious tradition. Each religion is associated with certain customs and religious practices. We use words such as 'liturgy' or 'ritual' to refer to some of the more stylized and established expressions of religion. Creedal statements of belief often serve to bind a community of faith in shared convictions, while the various traditions emphasize their own ways of dealing with life and death, good and evil, and the theological description of God or gods. Within the Christian tradition we can identify many common and recurrent themes, which by their broad acceptance define orthodoxy, while there is also tremendous diversity in the public expressions of faith. For the present purposes I want to refer to religion (unless specifically indicating otherwise) as the public expressions of the Christian faith, such as church services and related events, public meetings, crusades and gatherings, including those entered into through radio and other media.

'Spirituality' on the other hand, has a very different focus. For the present purpose, I use the term to refer to those personal experiences of God that may occur while in the company of others, yet more typically are associated with the private disciplines of prayer, fasting, reading the Scripture, etc. It is not uncommon for those with a strongly based personal spirituality to look disdainfully at public religious events as more superficial and, in a pejorative sense, 'merely religion'. Conversely, there are those who, while ready to attend public expressions of faith regularly and frequently (and hence seen by others to be religious) are at the same time underdeveloped in their personal experience of a relationship with God. It is not difficult to identify some Christian church traditions as placing a heavy emphasis on public liturgical expression of faith, while others downplay the formalities in order to stress the value of the intra-personal experience of faith.

We can therefore conclude that there are two different areas of experience represented by religion and spirituality respectively. Although ideally we could expect to find both equally valued during spiritual development, we cannot assume this will be so. It is important to address each of these two areas as if they were distinct, in order to consider ways in which hypnosis may relate to them.

Hypnosis and religion

It may at first sound shocking to suggest that public worship services are in any way related to hypnosis. Certainly, it is not a case of one person controlling another in a face-to-face encounter with a swinging watch and commanding the other to go to sleep. We may be prepared to admit that some do go to sleep anyway when the sermon goes on too long on a hot day. But if we take account of the reality of ASCs, rather than the false stereotype, we can more readily recognize aspects of public religion which at least have a lot in common with hypnosis; and many, if not most, regular worshippers will acknowledge an altered state.

Indeed, if we do not ever experience an ASC while in church, we may well be missing out on a central component of Christian worship. Those in the mystical tradition of the church will readily acknowledge such changes – such as the experience of St John on the Isle of Patmos who was in the Spirit on the Lord's Day (Rev. 1:10). Those in the charismatic tradition similarly experience, indeed welcome and facilitate, changes such that one can be oblivious of others around, intensely focused, and having a sense of detachment from the outer-world realities. This form of public worship perhaps has the most in common with entering into a hypnotic trance though, ironically, it is charismatic and Pentecostal pastors who are often among the strongest critics of hypnosis. Those from the liturgical traditions (Catholic, Episcopal, Lutheran, Orthodox) undoubtedly experience ASCs as a function of some of the liturgy itself, while the non-liturgical traditions such as the free-church evangelicals should not be ignored since, even though much in public services is propositional and kept in order, this is not the case as soon as we look at public evangelistic occasions.

With those broad-brush generalizations I hope I have not left too many readers out. Having sought to establish that ASCs are not what happens to someone else, it is worth looking at a few specifics arising from these traditions to illustrate the point. I was first alerted to these relationships by George Matheson's commentary on the evangelistic service or crusade, in which, without denying the spiritual significance and the real work of God in such events, he drew parallels between them and hypnotic experiences.[1] Looking across to the charismatic churches, Matheson referred to some earlier writing by Tappeiner who, in 1977,

> examined prophetical experience as currently manifested in many charismatic Christian churches and concluded that hypnagogic imagery seemed to be the mechanism by which the production of these utterances could be understood. Tappeiner acknowledged the divine source of these prophecies, but stressed that certain characteristics of the hypnagogic state, specifically vividness, originality, changefulness, and independence of conscious control, made it the most suitable channel for divine communications. Tappeiner attributed the reception of these non-logical utterances by the group to the worshipful format and the expectations of the participants.[2]

The liturgical tradition is characterized by a regular ritual service which, by its very familiarity, draws people together with shared expectations. The familiar words, the use of robes representing authority, the sequences of rhythm and quiet meditation, often in a darker-than-usual environment, aided sometimes by incense and other powerful sensory cues, together generate a uniquely powerful collective experience. In a

---

1 Matheson, 'Hypnotic aspects of religious experiences'.
2 ibid. p. 17.

presentation to her colleagues at a conference on hypnosis, a physician Dr Margaretta Bowers explored the relationship between hypnotic states and what happens in worship and prayer within both the Christian and Jewish traditions. She emphasized the need to identify the use to which an ASC may be put. 'In order to understand the potency of the hypnotic situation it is important to distinguish between hypnosis as a vehicle, and the hypnotic behavior that is induced by the suggestion that is explicit or implicit in the hypnotic situation, so that when hypnosis is used in the service of religion, the phenomenon of devotion in prayer and worship is to be expected.'[3]

A former student of mine, Dr. Tim Hogan, has written about such influences from within the Roman Catholic tradition, giving an account not only of specific components which show similarity to hypnotic inductions, but also of how the flow of events, as a ritual sequence, builds up to create a powerful impact during the celebration of the Mass. For example:

> There are many similarities between the ritual actions in the celebration of the Eucharist and the effective techniques of hypnosis. First, the physical environment of Catholic churches is designed so as to minimize distracting stimuli. The focus and centerpiece of the church is the altar, brightly-lit and usually elevated, with a crucifix suspended from the ceiling and the tabernacle at eye-level. The artwork on the side walls catches wandering eyes and gently signals them back to the theme of the celebration, the paschal mystery.[4]

He goes on to identify not only visual narrowing of attention, but also the impact of auditory and kinaesthetic cues, such as kneeling, walking forward, and participation in monotonous verbal exchanges. All prayers end with the same formula, all responses from the people are usually sung to the same melody. In some instances the priest chants the prayers, making this rhythm even more profound. Other signals are sometimes used to mark signal important events, such as incense before reading the Gospel and consecrating the bread and wine, and ringing bells during the consecration.[5]

Writing from his experience of the Seventh Day Adventist style of worship, Berecz reflects:

> One of my favorite pastors typically begins sermons with the following prayer, Oh, Lord, now as your people wait, let them hear only your voice. Let all other

---

[3] Bowers, M. K. (1959), 'Friend or traitor? Hypnosis in the service of religion', *International Journal of Clinical and Experimental Hypnosis*, 7, 205.

[4] Hogan, T. (1992), 'Hypnosis and the celebration of the Eucharist: Relationship and implications', paper presented to the Annual Convention, Christian Association of Psychological Studies (CAPS-West).

[5] ibid.

> voices be silent as you speak to us this morning. Then the pastor speaks for the next half hour. Unwittingly, I think both pastor and parishioners have entered into a hypnotic contract of sorts, that minimizes critical thinking and blurs the boundaries between the very human voice of the pastor and the divine voice of the Almighty God.[6]

Indeed, Charles Finney, in his *Lectures on revivals* in 1835, went further, not only drawing attention to the psychological phenomena that may be operating in evangelistic events, but proposing that the conversion process could actually be studied and enhanced to bring more powerful results. He 'outlined what he believed to be an empirically tested system of techniques designed to turn the conversion process into a lawful science. . . . Religious conversions were procured by a scientific application of natural laws, not a miraculous intervention of them. . . . Finney counseled that he who deals with souls should study well the laws of the mind'.[7]

While we do not need to dismiss the miraculous intervention of God in conversion, it is indisputably evident in these days of TV evangelism that techniques of influence are often exploited to gain support, response, and commitment. It is worth noting that, when at such times we experience significant changes of feeling and/or beliefs, we tend to attribute such changes externally: that is, effects are produced from without, and we most readily invoke God as the source of such changes. This can be an entirely appropriate attribution. Those who respond to an evangelistic appeal at a crusade often remark how they felt drawn to move rather than making a conscious choice. They sense a personal encounter with God which is irresistible. The involvement of trance-like phenomena does not invalidate the true significance of such a response, but does emphasize how altered states are part of normal human experience, and can be the vehicle for profound, even life-transforming change. Similarly, glossolalics who speak in tongues in public worship have the sense of utterances beyond their own conscious choices, and appear to be in an altered state at such times. That some people can and do demonstrate glossolalia more readily than others may well relate either to their capacity to dissociate, or their hypnotizability.[8]

These experiences of responding to the promptings of the Holy Spirit suggest that such altered states can be beneficial in enriching personal and

---

[6] Berecz, J. (1994), 'Hypnosis – Yes: SDAs should use it', *Spectrum, 23*, 4, 40.

[7] Quoted in R. C. Fuller (1982), *Mesmerism and the American cure of souls*. (Philadelphia: University of Pennsylvania Press), pp. 76–7.

[8] Malony, H. N. & Lovekin, A. A. (1985), *Glossolalia: Behavioral science perspectives on speaking in tongues*. (New York: Oxford University Press).

corporate religious experience. If such interpretations of what happens at public religious events should appear somehow irreverent or dismissive of the truly spiritual dimensions of such behaviour, I want not only to insist that this is not the case, but to illustrate why I am still asserting the validity of a religious interpretation.

With regard to those who make a public confession of faith at an evangelistic event, we cannot always assume that the response is a true conversion experience with lasting consequences. Every evangelist knows there are many who profess but then go no further. There are others who are 'repeat responders', feeling a strong compulsion to come forward at every appeal. It takes little effort to conclude that such people are responding not to a spiritual call but to inner psychological turmoil. The outward behaviour appears the same as in the true converts but the motivation is different.

So too where glossolalia are encouraged, giving rise to authentic expressions which are subject to interpretation. There are parallels with hypnosis, not only in the speaker's unselfconscious involvement which largely disregards other people close by, but also in the often-raised issue about control. Those unfamiliar with glossolalia may say, 'That's not for me. I don't want to lose control like that.' To this comes the response that it does not involve loss of control but rather a choice to hand over control to the moving of the Spirit. There always remains the choice to cease at any time, just as with the termination of hypnotic trance. In addition to the use of an unknown language (glossolalia), some individuals show a surprising ability to speak in a foreign language (xenoglossy), without prior exposure to it. While some have argued that this provides convincing proof of a past-life, a more rigorous approach to the data suggests that this ability may be related to possession rather than reincarnation in some cases, and the previous learning but subsequent forgetting (cryptomnesia) in others.[9]

Yet there are other counterfeit expressions which mimic the true gift. Glossolalia is not confined to the Christian charismatic community but is known the world over in other contexts. Hence, while the Spirit may enable some to be gifted in this way, there are others who, for other reasons, also speak in tongues. An ASC appears to be a common denominator for all such manifestations, Christian or not. The expression of glossolalia which is not of the Spirit need not automatically be dismissed

---

[9] See several studies by I. Stevenson, quoted by Venn, 'Hypnosis for Christians'.

as therefore demonic, but may rather be seen as the expression of an ASC based on the essentially normal phenomena of trance.

If these public religious events are the context for significantly altered states, in settings where authority is more readily accepted and suggestions are more powerful than at other times, then there is an ethical need for preachers, teachers, and healers to have a very clear understanding of these principles. It would be terribly easy to misinterpret what is happening when a person makes an affirmation of faith, or claims to be healed, since they could be the product of spurious high suggestibility. The hazards of manipulation and abuse of the power relationship are all too often apparent in American mass-media religion, but can be evident in smaller groupings too. The parallels with hypnotic phenomena can scarcely be denied, and the following caution deserves reflection:

> The religionist can no longer hide his head in the sand and claim ignorance of the science and art of the hypnotic discipline . . . whether he approves or disapproves, every effective religionist, in the usages of ritual, preaching and worship, unavoidably makes use of hypnotic techniques, and is therefore subject to the same responsibilities as known and acknowledged by the scientifically trained hypnotist.[10]

Identifying the hazards of hypnotically powerful influences in the religious context Rabbi Bertram Korn of Philadelphia once said:

> I shudder to think of the havoc wreaked by clergymen who utilize various counseling techniques without adequate control or comprehension. I suspect that hypnosis is an even more dangerous technique than others in the hands of the half-baked and half-trained. Clergymen possess a stupendous power over the minds and deeds of their adherents and followers; great devastation has come to man from the misguided proclamations of clergymen who have used their power without comprehending the inherent danger of their responsibility.[11]

Hypnosis and spirituality

Discussion of experiences within the public domain of religious expression leads naturally to consideration of ASCs in the more intimate experience of personal spirituality. Any who take seriously a commitment to extended prayer or meditation, and those who engage in fasting as a spiritual discipline, know that certain changes occur at these times.

---

[10] Bowers, 'Friend or traitor?'.

[11] Korn, B. W. (1964), *Religion and hypnosis meet*, Panel presentation to the Seventh Annual Meeting of the American Society of Clinical Hypnosis, Philadelphia, pp. 30–31.

While some of these changes are unique to each person, there are also many frequently reported changes which, in context, are accepted or welcomed as a component of the spiritual experience: a sense of distancing from the outside world, often to the point that external distractions are disregarded; an ability to focus intently on a picture or idea to enhance worship; the use of repetitive phrases such as 'Jesus is Lord', or 'Hallelujah' to enhance this focusing; and breathing patterns changed, deliberately or incidentally. These represent but a few of the changes that may be experienced. To those familiar with the features of hypnotic trance, such phenomena are consistent with trance-like states. Sometimes there are sensory changes such as the experience of a bright light, or the sense of a temperature change, as with John Wesley who reported being 'strangely warmed'.

Such changes are commonly associated with a significant sense of the closeness of God. For those who regularly practise the disciplines there is the sense of practising the presence of God so that he is recognized as ever-present. Others who are occasional in their dedication to times of prayer and fasting report that such times become high points of special closeness. In contrast to the experience of external compulsion in public religious settings, there is more a sense of internal concentration to the inner core of the self, as the presence of God is incorporated. As Matheson comments: 'When compared with "spiritual", religion is generally seen as having an external focus on practice and form. In contrast, the essence of spiritual is that of soul or life, immaterial and yet at the center of one's being.'[12]

There are many aspects of personal spiritual disciplines which show close similarities to the use of clinical hypnosis for relaxation and anxiety reduction. In private prayer many have a preferred physical position which is adopted – sitting, kneeling, prostrate, etc. Mostly there is an expression of being humble before God. In hypnosis it is usual to adopt a position of comfort and an attitude of passivity or receptiveness. There is a heightened level of expectation. It would fit well for a Christian using self-hypnosis to pray Samuel's prayer, 'Speak, Lord, for your servant is listening.'

Those who practise contemplative prayer speak of 'centring' as an important preparation. This is comparable to the dissociation from external events and focusing of attention, characteristic of the entry into hypnotic trance. According to Woods, mystical experiences include

---

[12] Matheson, 'Hypnosis', in Benner, *Baker encyclopedia of psychology*.

contemplation and renunciation with contemplation being the non-analytic grasping of an idea, and renunciation a focus on leaving worldly things behind. Contemplation involves tuning out stimuli in order to focus actively, yet at the same time requiring passive self-surrender. Renunciation seeks to ensure a focus not in self but on God. The profound and vivid experiences of the mystic bear a strong resemblance to the enriched imagery of the hypnotic state.

When engaging in active prayers of adoration and intercession, the issue of visual imagery is common if not universal. In spite of the warnings that have been offered regarding the use of visualization, and the suggestion that this is the province of New Age religion, in reality Christians have always used it, as have believers in Old Testament days. Although visual images often serve as helpful guides to effective prayer, we can also draw from the hypnotic literature[13] the importance of other kinds of imagery, the two most common additions being auditory and kinaesthetic, or sounds and touch. Most of us imagine (that is, construct images) using predominantly visual or auditory material; a few find themselves most at ease with the sense of touch. The richest development of our imagination occurs when we can incorporate all three. It is not difficult to find in the Psalms and in contemporary hymns many indications of the use of these senses in prayer and worship. Psalm 63, for example, is richly metaphorical with allusions to various senses, and was one of the psalms used in daily public prayers by the early church. It is an expression of intense longing to experience God's presence:

> O God, you are my God,
> Earnestly I seek for you;
> My soul thirsts for you,
> My body longs for you. . .
> I have seen you in the sanctuary. . .
> I will lift up my hands. . .
> With singing lips my mouth will praise you.

There is here a full involvement of body and senses in this expression of worship. A current song incorporating visual and touch sensations runs:

> I want to see Jesus
> I want to reach out and touch Him

and of course many such songs refer to listening for God's voice in some way.

---

[13] Especially Bandler, R. & Grinder, J. (1979), *Frogs into princes, (Moab, UT: Real People Press);* Lankton, S. (1983), *The answer within: A clinical framework of Ericksonian hypnotherapy* (New York: Brunner/Mazel).

In singing such songs there is no suggestion of hallucinating the presence of Jesus, or expecting a physical manifestation. Yet it expresses a yearning for a significant spiritual experience which allows us all to participate through the three dimensions of seeing, hearing and touching. To experience the close presence of Jesus is one of the most meaningful spiritual experiences. Those who practise centering prayer and allow undisturbed time for this can testify to the effectiveness of these disciplines. Similarly these rich experiences can be explored within the hypnotic trance. Often, when working with traumatic memories, I have asked clients, 'Would you like to have someone with you as you deal with this again,' and not infrequently they indicate they want Jesus included. At such times it is not unusual to have a more powerful and more comforting experience of the presence of Jesus than they have known before, with a subsequent strengthening of faith. It is possible to ask people at such times, 'What does Jesus look like?' and a very clear description can be provided – not describing, as if by magic, an appearance of the historical Jesus, but rather a representation which is based on prior experience and with attributes relevant to the individual's needs.

The potential for close relationship between hypnotic techniques and spiritual aspirations was discussed some years ago by an ecumenical group at a conference sponsored by the American Society of Clinical Hypnosis. In that context, J. J. Higgins, a Roman Catholic professor of education from St Louis University, said:

> My own point of view, and it coincides with that of the Roman Catholic Church, is that hypnosis is very useful and there is no objection to its use, provided it is not attributed to any evil spirits or supernatural influence . . . I find the greatest use for hypnosis in addition to counseling, in teaching concentration and mental prayer. There are tremendous possibilities in this area. When we are dealing with intangibles, with eternal and spiritual life, with heaven and hell, we still have to use our reason and our mental powers to make contact with these ideas.[14]

A physician, J. W. Dorman, who taught women to use hypnosis in childbirth has found that a blending with spiritual aspirations can be most helpful. The closer bonding of therapist and patient generates a good deal of emotional sharing that goes beyond the procedures and practice of medicine as a science. He reports on a letter written to him saying: 'As I have thought back on the hypnosis classes, I have realized what wonderful thoughts you gave us in them, planting deep in the subconscious the

---

[14] *Religion and Hypnosis Meet* (1965), Panel discussion, American Society of Clinical Hypnosis Proceedings, Des Plaines, IL, pp. 28–9.

naturalness and beauty of God's plan for women to give birth and the perfect way in which he created our bodies to do this.'[15]

If there are parallels with prayer, then how much more so with fasting. This spiritual discipline is clearly one in which physiological changes occur and are deliberately induced. Reduced blood sugar brings changes to cerebral functioning such that care has to be exercised to avoid excessive effects leading to loss of consciousness. The change of metabolism is an adjunct to enhanced spirituality, having been valued for centuries, and of course practised by Jesus in his fasting. This discipline of the appetites induces an ASC which facilitates spiritual awareness. Physiological change is also among the more impressive demonstrations of the effectiveness of hypnosis. Changes in cardiovascular functioning, in immune system activity and control of the autonomic nervous system generally are now routinely taught to assist in the development of better health. Often this is linked to visualization (e.g. 'see the cancer shrinking' or 'watch the area of pain reducing') and can have valuable long-term effects.

If there are indeed such parallels, how can it be that Christians advocate one mode of healing and have such anxieties about the other? It is easy to see how two quite opposite things can be divided, with one good and one evil, but here we have too much overlap between spiritual disciplines and hypnosis to make such a convenient distinction.

The matter may be resolved by distinguishing the process from the purpose. We assume in the Christian tradition that to be prayerful and to fast are ways in which we seek to develop our relationship with God and to grow spiritually as children of God. To that extent we identify those practises as good. However, it is entirely possible to engage in the same activities (process) for very different ends (purpose). The inversions of faith seen in Satanism, with the use of incantation and religious practises which are calculated to mimic but distort Christian practices, provide striking evidence that what matters is not whether we pray but to whom or to what we pray. The same distinction can be made in relation to the world's religions generally, including New Age practises. There is acknowledgement of the powerful effectiveness of meditation and fasting, but the purpose to which these are put is different from the Christian application.

Coming from the other direction, hypnosis is thought to be dangerous by those who have seen its use for unhealthy or dangerous purposes. Kurt Koch provided a wise caution to the church after witnessing the use of

---

[15] Dorman, J. W. (1967), 'Spiritual resources in hypnosis', presentation to the Tenth Annual Meeting of the American Society of Clinical Hypnosis, Des Plaines, IL.

hypnosis within the rituals of Asian religions, attesting the tremendous influence obtained over people's beliefs and behaviour in this way.[16] We should not be surprised if a therapist who holds New Age beliefs encourages visualization exercises congruent with that world view. If hypnosis proves more effective than alternatives it will naturally be selected. Yet we have seen that the process can also lead to an authentic spiritual experience when used by, and with, Christians. Where the purpose is to know God, to understand God's truth, and to be more attuned to what may be God's purpose for us, why would we walk away from something which can help us along in that direction? Its abuse by others, or its use for different purposes, does not provide an adequate reason to discard hypnosis altogether.

This kind of distinction may be found with Dr Klaus Thomas who, from a background both as a psychiatrist and Lutheran pastor, has remarked that: 'In deepened prayer, in visualization and in the experience of the truth of the Bible outside of the intellect, there are similar states as a consequence of prayer and deepened meditation but not as the aim. There are states of consciousness here equivalent to those brought about by hypnosis, but not intentionally induced as in this, the result, rather than the aim. I use hypnosis every day as a psychiatrist, and self-hypnosis, and I find the same observation and the same state as the consequence of prayer . . .'[17]

If prayer can be considered as an altered state of consciousness, then what about speaking in tongues (or glossolalia)? There appear to be two views, with some saying an altered state is always present, while others believe this is sometimes the case, but not necessarily so. Malony and Lovekin, who explored the subject from a behavioural science perspective, distinguish between the two words 'trance' and 'possession', which are both terms used to describe an altered state but are not interchangeable terms: 'Trance is the phenomenon observed from the outside, whereas possession is the experience reported from the inside.'[18] They proceed to argue that it is possible for trance to occur with or without possession, and consider that glossolalia always involves possession, but not necessarily a trance state. The sense in which possession is used here is the theological proposition that tongues-speaking among Christians flows from possession (or in-filling) by the Holy Spirit. Such an experience may be

---

16 Koch, K. (1972), *Christian counseling and occultism* (Michigan: Kregel).

17 Thomas, K. (1964), *Religion and hypnosis meet.* Panel presentation to the Seventh Annual Meeting of the American Society of Clinical Hypnosis, Philadelphia, p. 34.

18 Malony & Lovekin, 'Glossolalia', p. 98.

associated with a changed sense of reality (an altered state), but this does not always occur. Malony and Lovekin sought out the opinions of some leading charismatics, such as Dennis Bennett and Michael Harper who 'have insisted that their glossolalia did not involve loss of consciousness and in spite of the fact that they attest to their ability to determine when and whether they express their "gift", the very essence of the experience has always been the presumption that one is taken over by the Holy Spirit and, thus, become *possessed* in a way that can be seen by anyone who is present'.[19]

If glossolalia always involves possession but not necessarily trance, then hypnosis may be understood as always involving trance, but not necessarily possession. Possession is not a scientific term, but comes from a theological interpretation of behaviour, whether it refers to the Christian experience of the Holy Spirit, or to the manifestations seen in other religions, where demonic influences are invoked. Hence the secular therapist using hypnosis for healing will be using the trance experience as a vehicle for therapy, without invoking the concept of possession. The Christian therapist might use it in the same way, but it could also be the opportunity for the client to experience the work of the Holy Spirit more freely if this is something to which they are already open.

Summary

This chapter has argued that there are a number of parallels between what happens in public religious practices, in private spirituality, and in hypnosis. The induction of an ASC is not accidental or incidental in the expression of faith, but quite central and to be valued. The shift from immediate reality to the transcendental appears to occur when we engage in spiritual disciplines, while collectively we are more responsive when the environment is such that we can experience an ASC. These shifts can be welcomed as part of the normal transition enabling us to focus our attention effectively.

So too with hypnosis. While significant therapeutic changes can occur without it, there is a facilitating effect such that people can choose change more readily than at other times. For the Christian there does not have to be an arbitrary dividing line between spiritual experiences and hypnotic phenomena, since the former can be enriched by the latter. Beyond the

[19] ibid. p. 97.

therapeutic advantages of hypnosis, it is also possible for hypnosis to enrich our spiritual experience and develop a fuller appreciation of the close presence of God in our lives.

Chapter 6

Hypnosis and Inner Healing

I have suggested in the preceding chapter that there are parallels between hypnotic experiences and those public aspects of Christian living which we call religious, as well as those more personal experiences embraced by the term spirituality. I have proposed that the normal shifts of consciousness, which can occur in private or public, enhance the possibility of enriching our spiritual responsiveness, as those shifts take us from the logical, pragmatic modes of experience towards a different kind of responding, more allied with sensitivity and creative reconstruction of experience. We should also note that such shifts of consciousness are characterized by a greater capacity to experience emotions (or perhaps a reduction in the tendency to inhibit emotions). That is, the experience of joy under normal circumstances may be greatly amplified in the hypnotic trance just as the experience of fear, anger and other negative emotions can also be more powerfully felt.

This understanding has existed since the early 1980s,[1] and its basis is being increasingly related to the shift of function during hypnosis from the left to the right hemisphere of the brain, and in particular to electrical rhythms with a frequency of 40 Hertz, which are associated with the physiological expression of focused arousal. Indeed, there are indications that people who are classified as high on hypnotizability not only access their emotions more readily while in a trance, but also at other times during normal consciousness.[2] This naturally leads back to a consideration of the similarities to be found between the clinical uses of hypnosis and spiritual interventions that seek to bring healing.

---

[1] See, for example, Bower, S. G., Gilligan, G. E. & Monteiro, K. P. (1981), 'Selectivity of learning caused by affective states', *Journal of Experimental Psychology, 110*, 451–73.

[2] See, for example, de Pascalis, V. & Marucci, F. S., '40-Hz EEG and focused attention: Implications for the study of hypnosis', XXV International Congress of Psychology, Brussels, 1992.

The existence of specific brain rhythms associated with emotional arousal suggests that these could be increased or decreased by a variety of interventions – through centrally-acting drugs, through hypnosis, and through other strategies which can evoke such physiological changes.

The long history of religious rituals designed to bring about alterations of consciousness provides evidence that there are common elements which can be used effectively, either alone or in groups. The use of deep breathing, sensory isolation, adoption of certain body postures, frenzied dancing, rhythmic music, especially drumming, and repetition of phrases (mantras) are examples of ways to enter a trance state. The use of drugs is also a frequent part of tribal trance inductions. Using such methods, native healers or shamans, have long been accepted as those who not only have spiritual leadership but also bring healings where modern medicine is not available.

This overlap in the functions of priests and physicians was well established, also in the Christian tradition, until the emergence of modern medicine and the separation of functions into the spiritual and the physical. The division of responsibilities, linked to a dualistic view that body and spirit are separate, led to a rather mechanistic approach by medicine and surgery, and an 'other-worldly' separation by the church away from its earlier healing ministry.

The tide is now flowing back again to recognize the overlap of these areas, and the possibilities for healing by spiritual interventions as well as by physical means. In the meantime, the rise of psychological awareness has brought in the third area of emotional healing. It is no longer possible to identify one approach to healing as the only one, nor to separate out the various approaches from one another.

A particularly interesting area of overlap is that of hypnosis, coming from the background of clinical therapies, and inner healing, coming from the background of spiritual interventions. Those involved in the inner healing movement in the church would not generally welcome the suggestion of a close parallel with hypnosis, since the latter is so often seen as tainted, yet observation of both does readily identify a great deal of similarity, and deserves some comparative assessment.[3]

---

[3] The following section is an adaptation of material I first published in 'Hypnosis and inner healing'. Reprinted here with permission.

Differing viewpoints on hypnosis and inner healing

Hypnosis, as we have seen, when clinically utilized, typically involves a state of deep relaxation. It includes an altered state of consciousness in which it is possible to focus attention, achieve enhanced recall of past experiences, and experience powerful emotions freed from defence mechanisms that otherwise block out past pain. Although patients often express a fear that they will lose control to their therapists, the reverse is probably closer to the truth. As they deal with their past experiences in hypnosis patients may be guided and offered suggestions by therapists, but the guidance and suggestions can be received or rejected by the patients' free choice; individuals ultimately achieve increased control of areas of their lives which were previously unknown to them, even destructive.

In the hypnotic state there is undoubtedly a shift from the primacy of reason toward an intensified awareness of emotional content. Simultaneously with the resurgence of interest in hypnosis among therapists from many schools, there has been a burgeoning interest in what is called 'healing of memories' or inner-healing prayer. We have witnessed the development of an innerhealing movement that originates from within the church and is based on a conviction that the Holy Spirit has power to heal. Hypnosis and inner healing, although based on different assumptions, nonetheless converge on the human problems involving emotions and past trauma and the search for healing from negative experiences.

There are multiple viewpoints within Christianity regarding the interplay of hypnosis and inner healing. Christian hypnotherapists indicate that hypnosis is a legitimate tool for therapy,[4] and when these clinicians compare hypnosis and inner healing they discover a parallel between them, especially when the focus is on experiences that involve affect and imagery.[5] Some Christian authors view these two healing approaches as essentially one and the same process, with any apparent differences being only superficial. At the opposite end of the spectrum,

---

[4] Court, 'Hypnosis revisited. Morton, *Hypnosis and pastoral counseling*. Newbold, 'Hypnotherapy and Christian belief'. Shepperson, V. L. (1981), 'Paradox, parables, and change: One approach to Christian hypnotherapy', *Journal of Psychology and Theology*, *9*, 1, 3–11; Shepperson, V. L. (1985), 'Hypnotherapy', in Benner, *Baker encyclopedia of psychology*. Venn, 'Hypnosis for Christians'.

[5] Matheson, G. (1979), 'Hypnotic aspects of religious experiences', *Journal of Psychology and Theology*, 7, 1, 13–21.

some go so far as to condemn all hypnosis as demonic and to be avoided at all costs[6].

The possibility that I espouse is that the phenomena are similar, that there are important differences, and that they complement one another. This conclusion may have some basis in the fact that hypnotherapists generally are moving away from the directive, authoritarian approach of earlier times toward a more flexible and indirect approach.[7] This newer, more flexible approach, with its liberal use of metaphor, analogy and age regression, has a great deal in common with the practice of both guided imagery and inner healing.[8]

Clinical experience

My experience with a number of clients leads me to the view that not only are the procedures of inner healing and hypnotherapy very similar, but they also can be complementary. In the inner healing approach of MacNutt, as described by Malony, in order to identify the painful emotion and its root, 'Before the prayer for healing is offered, two questions are explored with the person. First, when can you remember first feeling that way? Second, what was happening that caused you to feel that way?'[9]

By comparison, in hypnotherapy it is common to use the affect-bridge technique[10] for the same purpose. This approach, derived from psychoanalytic therapy, involves linking current experiences with events from the past in which the affective reaction in the present is seen as a reactivation of affect for past events. The client is asked to identify a negative affect, amplify it, and then recall the first experience of that affect. This often takes the client back to early childhood experiences that have not been susceptible to conscious recall. Description of the circumstances often is associated with a high level of affect, with significant relief

---

[6] e.g. Bobgan, M. & D. (1984), *Hypnosis and the Christian* (Minneapolis, MN:. Bethany House).

[7] Haley, J. (ed), (1967), *Advanced techniques of hypnosis and therapy* (New York: Grune and Stratton).

[8] Leuner, H. (1969), 'Guided affective imagery', *American Journal of Psychotherapy, 23*, 4–22. Short, J. E. (1983), *Psychotherapy through imagery* (New York: Thieme Stratton). Matheson, 'Hypnotic aspects of religious experiences'; Shepperson, 'Paradox, parables and change','Hypnotherapy'. *Baker encyclopedia of psychology*.

[9] Malony, H. N. (1985), 'Inner healing' in Benner.

[10] Watkins, 'The affect bridge'.

following. In addition to the affective experience, the events of the past also are brought forward so that the adult client can bring adult insight to bear on these early events.

For the inner healer, 'If the person cannot remember an incident, then God is asked to reveal it. After the time and place of the hurt has been identified, a prayer for the healing of the hurt is offered. In as imaginative and childlike a manner as possible, the healer prays that Jesus will go back into the experience and heal the person of the wound that resulted from it.'[11] This revelation may occur within the memory of the client, or may arise through a gift of discernment in the healer.

In both inner healing and hypnosis it is clear that cognitive processes of perception, memory, and imagination are focused and utilized. In addition, it is clear that both approaches assume that the cognitive experience alone is not enough for healing to occur. The re-experiencing of the early event together with the relevant affect is an integral part of the therapeutic process.[12] Matheson, writing about healing of memories, says:

> Through methods of reappraisal and prayer, he [the client] resolves the hurt and/or achieves cathartic release through an abreactive process. The clear similarity of this procedure to the psychoanalytic method is evident and unmistakable. The induction of hypnosis and its implementation in retracing the memory (through a technique similar to Watkins', 1971, 'affect bridge') is undeniably obvious, and a crucial variable in the undertaking.[13]

Hence, in both techniques there is a return to earlier experiences, with the use of imagery. In both cases the combination of affect and reason is sought to bring relief, but, in addition, in inner healing the events are given over to Jesus for healing. My observation of a number of clients who have received prayer for healing and then hypnotherapy has made it clear to me that the experience of clients can be very similar in both contexts; indeed, one approach can facilitate the other. At times it is not easy to differentiate one mode from the other, as when, for example, a prayerful person who also is highly hypnotizable has been taught self-hypnosis. In such an instance it appears that the techniques of hypnosis can be used to enhance prayerful inner healing. The combination of prayerful meditation using techniques taught in hypnosis without the therapist's intervention can enhance the direct relationship with God, confirming that control remains with the client.

---

[11] Malony, 'Inner healing'.

[12] Seamands, D. A. (1985), *Healing of memories* (Wheaton, IL: Victor Books).

[13] Matheson, 'Hypnotic aspects of religious experiences', p. 19.

Example

In the following example, which illustrates this relationship, my client had first received significant benefit within a prayer-healing context and then developed her own ministry to others. She presented with some residual yet still incapacitating problems that were significantly relieved after working through the re-experiencing of an attempted rape. That event had not been discerned by her prayer healer, and she had not mentioned it to him. It was available to conscious recall when I took her history, which follows.

SESSION 1

A single female, whom I will call Brenda, aged forty-four, presented following a phone call from a friend who had recommended that she seek further help for depression. Brenda presented as a person of medium height and appropriate weight, lively in appearance but negative in her verbal content. The initial account she gave of herself was of being a failure, a person with very low self-esteem and currently quite unable to cope. She had resigned from work four-and-a-half months previously, and hoped she might eventually recover enough to get back to a less stressful type of work. She reported: 'Some days I am so lethargic I have slept and slept. I feel there must be something better than antidepressants.'

Brenda's father was fifty-one when she was born. Chronically depressive and sexually frustrated, he died at the age of seventy-one of a heart attack after six years of physical ill health. Brenda commented: 'I grieved intensely for one week.' Her mother suffered motor-neuron disease requiring nursing by Brenda until she died, when Brenda was thirty-three.

She developed amenorrhoea at fifteen, and this condition persisted for twenty years. She was very thin and wondered in retrospect whether she had an undiagnosed case of anorexia nervosa. Having stayed home until she was thirty-three, ostensibly to nurse a sick mother, she said she had chosen 'unsuitable boyfriends' and related to them in such a way as to avoid deeper levels of intimacy. She then moved into a job in television which involved her in high-stress situations and demanded challenging schedules which she enjoyed enormously.

She became a Christian when she was thirty-five, at which time her menstrual periods returned, and she experienced an improvement in her life adjustment. She changed jobs to work with a charitable organization as an office supervisor. Later, however, she left this job because the work was 'too stressful'; she also was suffering dyspepsia and depression. The dyspepsia cleared up when she left this position, but the depression continued, and when seen by me she was unemployed.

For the previous five years she had been involved in a prayer-healing group at her local church. She experienced five years of healing prayer for herself and assisted in prayer for others. She reported that these prayer experiences had been most helpful in dealing with many of her traumatic early memories, notably of sexual molestation at age eight by a male neighbour.

Brenda also reported an attempted rape when she was aged thirty-three, following which she had a 'nervous breakdown', leading to her use of antidepressants ever since. She reported with a rather surprised look that this latter episode had not come up as a focus for prayer healing. At this time she obtained the clinically significant score of 19 on the Beck Depression Inventory, including the response, 'I feel that the future is hopeless and cannot improve.'

SESSION 2

During Brenda's second visit, hypnosis was induced and she gave the following explanation. After being invited to find a safe place, she described playing in the street with her brother when she was ten – 'the last time I was happy'. When asked to retrieve another childhood experience, she recalled her mother's anger: 'She was always angry with me . . . I shouldn't have been around . . . She didn't want me as a girl.' She believed her mother's anger and rejection expressed a wish that her daughter should not grow up to be a woman and she related this to her subsequent amenorrhoea. 'I stopped menstruation at fifteen . . . no one cared.' At this point in the hypnotic session she became physically cold, with cyanosis of the fingers, and was close to tears. She spoke of re-experiencing 'aloneness' and 'emptiness' at this point in the session. She accepted the suggestion of Jesus countering her aloneness and emptiness and bringing her warmth. I remained silent in the background, observing her responses. (Often in such circumstances I will offer a Scripture verse for meditation, but in this instance I did not.) Left undisturbed, Brenda warmed up over about a ten-minute period. Before the session ended, I arranged for her to maintain close contact with her pastor and his wife in case of need before the next counseling appointment. She said she anticipated that she would do some crying at home.

SESSION 3

Brenda's next visit took place three days later: it was planned so soon after her first visit in light of her distress level. She described the day after her previous visit as a 'write-off'. Although she was unsuccessful initially in her attempts, she eventually did weep. As she had wept alone, I reminded her again of the need and value of seeking support from her trusted pastor and his wife.

She briefly described the experience of being molested at age eight by the father of a friend, saying, 'This has been dealt with in prayer counselling.' She seemed to indicate that the incident needed no further mention. 'But always there was terror in my childhood, even in the very early years.' In hypnosis, I asked her to go back to 'the earliest time that you can recall'. She then described being in the kitchen at her home when she was about three years old. 'Aloneness. Mummy is sleeping and can't help. She doesn't know what I want.' I asked, 'What is that?' and Brenda replies, 'Love.' This event was noted but not pursued further at the time. After the hypnotic state had ended, she said, 'I've always had the feeling something happened in the kitchen. . . . She's put me in the kitchen so she wouldn't hear me cry.' I then picked up on her earlier use of the word terror and asked her to experience this with amplified intensity. Then, with the help of an affect bridge, she went back to age eight and achieved revivification of being in the dentist's chair. That is, she vividly experienced this real event from her past. 'Crying and crying . . . no one tells me what will happen . . . my mother is angry because I am causing trouble.' Asked to describe the dentist, she replied, 'Frightening, cold, a big man.' 'What does he look like?' A pregnant pause followed, then she said, 'He looks like my friend's father,' i.e. the man who had molested her a short time before. She readily accepted that her terror was a conditioned fear, and said afterward, 'I don't need that fear any more, do I?' During that revivification there was a good deal of abreaction. As we talked through the meaning of her experience, I endeavoured to make explicit for her the link between her dental fear and her fear when molested. According to her report, she then left my office feeling unusually calm.

SESSION 4

At Brenda's next visit she reported having watched the television movie *Sybil* at a friend's home. She said it was 'stupid' to have watched it because a prior viewing had previously led her to seek prayer counselling. It activated many of her early memories and fears, especially of the manipulative control of a girl by her mother. The fear of being controlled was identified as a recurrent and central theme in her problems. Apart from that experience, she said, 'I'm more optimistic this last three weeks.' Although she had been making inquiries about taking a job, she said, 'I'm a total failure.'

Challenged by me along the lines of Beck's cognitive therapy to look at why she had left her previous job, she reported that it was not merely because of stress but also because of 'sexual harassment from the boss'. This proved to be more imagined than real, but fitted her view that she was under someone else's control. We reviewed assertiveness techniques,[14] noting that her difficulty in saying no to these requests related to her fear of failure and loss of approval. The major task of this session was to confront her belief in her own helplessness in favour of an acceptance of self-efficacy.

SESSION 5

Brenda reported, 'I've got over the failure bit' since she had been visiting an employment agency to get a 'small job'. Before hypnosis, she had commented, 'I wrote an essay recently and realized that fear controlled my whole life.' It is worthwhile noting here that initially she had been fearful of hypnosis, knowing that in trance we would be exploring together the fearful events of her past. After careful explanation on my part, and development of a relationship of trust with me, she agreed to the hypnotic approach because I emphasized that she would be more in control under hypnosis than at other times when she was simply fearful, and that we also would create a safe place to which she could go at any time. With this careful preparation, Brenda eventually became a ready subject for the hypnotic process.

Her revivification of her friend's father molesting her led to an abreactive response. As she re-experienced her terror, feeling threatened and alone, I suggested that she might become aware of the presence of Jesus, recognizing that he had been there, unnoticed, all the time. She easily accepted the awareness of his presence as a source of comfort. Anxiety was progressively replaced by peace and reflectiveness.

---

[14] Sanders, R. D. & Malony, H. N. (1985), *Speak up: Christian assertiveness* (Philadelphia: Westminster Press).

SESSION 6

Brenda reported crying on and off for thirty-six hours after her last visit. Ideally this should have occurred with the comfort and presence of others. In spite of my earlier encouragements to call on others for support, her timidity and fear kept her from asking for companionship and resulted in her being alone with her tears. This was neither necessary nor desirable. However, at this time she agreed to recall, in my presence, the attempted rape experience she had at age thirty-three.

Revivification of this event occurred with great emotion regarding having a man enter her room, her screaming, his assault, her fear of having 'no one to help me', and her escape to a neighbour's flat two doors away. Initially, she reported anger at the intruder. As we proceeded, over a period of about half an hour, she was encouraged to release this emotional reaction, allowing it to be transformed so that she could see the attacker as a man with serious problems, someone for whom she could feel sorrow or pity. Throughout this process we asked for Jesus' help in her adopting a forgiving spirit. She even became thankful because, as the man had entered her room, he had scraped a chair and this noise had alerted her before he had reached her so that she was able to resist and escape. I encouraged her to see the value of doing the hard work of transforming her negative recollections into attitudes of forgiveness and thankfulness.

SESSION 7

Brenda reported that she was now sleeping well. However, the anxiety continued. She said, 'I feel the trauma has gone from my stomach to my brain.' We agreed to use hypnotic regression again and return to her memory of being in the kitchen of her childhood home. She had previously identified the importance of this memory from when she was very young, but at the time of recall we no more than simply noted her loneliness. That very early sense of lacking parental affection needed attention. With revivification, she described being eighteen months old and in her cot, 'very alone', with her parents sleeping. She was put into the kitchen so they could not hear her. With minimal direction she reconstructed her experience, with Jesus picking her up from the cot, comforting her, and putting her back down to sleep peacefully.

SESSION 8

She introduced the session by smiling broadly at me, saying, 'I have been healed. It's happened!' She had been routinely buying the paper to search for a job, and had visited her general practitioner to say, 'I don't want any more sick leave.' To me she said that 'sleep is marvellous'. Further exploration revealed that Brenda was experiencing only minimal difficulties with depression and a knot in the stomach, due to fear of the unknown.

Once again she completed the Beck Depression Inventory, this time with a score of 10 (within normal limits). She planned to remain on a minimal dose of antidepressants for a while, in consultation with her local doctor.

DISCUSSION

Brenda came with high expectations and confidence, although experiencing serious, chronic depression. She had received significant help previously through prayer healing, but some areas of trauma had remained unresolved. Hypnotic techniques enabled her to access and deal with several episodes from her childhood and a major adult trauma.

Her extreme depressive response regarding the future moved from 8 to 0 on the final assessment. She was preparing to re-enter the work force and was speaking positively of herself and her abilities. Initially she had felt uncertain about the acceptability of hypnosis as a legitimate therapeutic method because of doubts expressed by other Christians. In addition, she wondered whether, even if hypnotherapy were acceptable, it could really achieve what had not been achieved through prayer healing.

Once I reassured her regarding the first point, she was ready to proceed. Her first powerful abreaction was sufficient to convince her that there were, indeed, areas that had not been resolved adequately before. Her confidence and expectations increased, and her depression was reduced. At this time of writing, all goals for therapy have been met. She has obtained work and coped well for several years. A few issues remain that are likely to require occasional counselling, but it is unlikely that further deep exploration will be necessary.

Conclusions

This case illustrates the use of hypnosis within a Christian framework and its similarity to inner healing work. Brenda had previously experienced a considerable amount of spiritual ministry with substantial benefit, yet residual problems remained. A background of extensive healing prayer provided a good basis for continuing in her own healing process. There were several previously untouched areas of her life that she was able to deal with, and, within the trance state, she was able to experience a powerful sense of Jesus' presence in her times of need. From that, in a remarkably short interval, she was able to move into forgiveness of others, and an experience of peace herself.

The techniques of hypnosis were applied and they took her into spiritually significant experiences. The affect bridge was used in the conventional way to identify, amplify, and go back to early emotional experiences. Instead of bringing adult rationality to bear at this point, I used the technique of bringing Jesus into the experiences and thereafter dealt with them as one might do in healing prayer.

I see no need to argue whether hypnosis is better or worse than healing prayer. Rather, what seems important to me is that therapists develop their God-given gifts. The present case suggests that prayer healing will not necessarily deal with all the areas needing to be resolved. One may conjecture that an extended or even more skilful use of healing prayer would have achieved complete resolution, but it is sufficient to say that Brenda had come as far as she believed she could when involved in this process. Hypnosis too has its limitations. It is only a technique, and the extent to which it is therapeutic depends a great deal on the ways the trance state is used. Hypnosis can be powerful in bringing about cognitive change and in the management of psychosomatic disorders. In the present context I would argue that the hypnotic state is also well-suited to the incorporation of the spiritual resources of prayer, meditation, and the healing experience of Jesus' presence.

In both healing prayer and hypnosis heightened affect is usual but not essential to the therapeutic experience *per se*. The work of the Holy Spirit is crucial for healing to take place, as healing is from God. However, though the work of the Holy Spirit is not assumed to be necessary for hypnosis; it is neither to be discarded. The prayerful therapist can be guided in hypnotherapy as in any other form of therapy. With inner healing, there is commonly an emphasis on discernments made by the healer, who identifies areas where the Spirit can work. With hypnosis, it is usual to allow clients to explore their own experiences without external promptings.

One advantage of hypnosis was brought to my attention by a client some years ago. She had received a good deal of healing ministry, often lasting for hours at a time, and was subsequently introduced to hypnosis. Asked about the differences she said 'Under hypnosis, you can look at something very painful and emotional which really hurts. Then you can leave it and not take the pain with you. I still know what we have talked about afterwards but I can leave the pain behind because it has been dealt with at a different level. Some prayer counselors touch on hypnosis without realizing it. That scares me more because they don't know how to leave it. I respect prayer counselling for what it is, but it's different. The hurt walks out through the door with me and then I can't cope.'[15] In an exploratory way, I suggest that these two approaches, far from being in opposition, are best seen as complementary, to be used according to our gifts and skills.

[15] Quoted in 'Hypnotism', *New Day International* (May 1988), 9.

Chapter 7

Hypnosis, Exorcism and Healing

Concerns that hypnosis may somehow have powerful and dangerous links to religious practices are not new. Indeed, these beliefs have a good deal of history behind them, both in the Western world and in other cultures.

Hypnosis as we know it today, used professionally by many therapists, has direct links back to the work of Anton Mesmer (1734–1815) whose name gave us the term 'Mesmerism', and before him we find religious roots in the practices of exorcism in the church. Although mesmerism is the term by which the man is remembered, he is better understood for his development of what came to be known as 'animal magnetism'[1] since this was the theoretical explanation that he offered for what he did. If we understand something of Mesmer's approach, and the assault launched upon it by those from the worlds of science and religion, we shall appreciate more fully what the issues are that now surround the use of hypnosis.

Within this historical context it will also not come as any surprise that, for centuries, many Christians have experienced ambivalence or mistrust regarding hypnosis (and its earlier forms under different names). If the tension were simply the conflicting claims of science versus religion the issues might be clear-cut, and the debate that has surrounded these two might embrace hypnosis as one example of this. It is true that there has been such a tension, but that is only the beginning.

Within the domain of religious thought there have also been tensions. Many of the phenomena of hypnosis, and the uses to which they are put, have been identified and used by the church in dealing with possession states and demonic manifestations. The Catholic Church in particular had a strong commitment to the practice of exorcism, and the identification

---

[1] See Laurence & Perry, *Hypnosis, will and memory*.

of many behavioural abnormalities with the work of the devil. Other churches, seeking to minimize the role of the devil, were keen to dismiss such teaching as superstitious and medieval, so that church leaders themselves were divided in their response to this apparently scientific development which challenged their spiritual view of the world. A related tension, with spiritual implications, arose from the move by heterodox believers to incorporate the new understandings of hypnosis into their practices, and in particular make this a core component of the Christian Scientists. This endorsement by spiritualism naturally caused others in the mainstream church to be very wary.

On the scientific front the tensions were perhaps more divisive as the newly emerging criteria for determining scientific proof were used to evaluate the claims made by eighteenth-century practitioners. Throughout the eighteenth and nineteenth centuries a major transition was occurring in which the definitions of healing were being reviewed, as well as the definitions of who would be regarded by society as the legitimate healers.[2]

The central role of the church, with an understanding of sickness defined in terms of God, the devil, and sin, was modified as medical science became increasingly effective in finding cures which made no such assumptions. The status of the medical practitioner increased as that of the priest declined. Yet that simple equation fails to recognize the many other groups who were laying claim to the healing arts. There had always been the quacks and charlatans who developed brief followings, and moved on. But it was the emergence of 'animal magnetism,' a development of the 'magnetic medicine' which had been practised since the fifteenth century, which brought another set of tensions – between those seen as legitimate practitioners using conventional medical knowledge, and their colleagues within the field medicine who insisted on this striking and apparently powerful alternative, resembling religious practices but applied to medical conditions.

Some of the eddies and currents of this historical river deserve summary here in order to create a context for what follows. As if the major external tensions were not great and complex enough, their attempted resolution was made much more difficult by at least two additional forces. Firstly, the individuals involved in the historical emergence of hypnosis brought their own personalities, beliefs and affiliations to the task. Public and private rivalries, allegations and

---

2 This transition is explored in Podmore, F. (1909), *From Mesmer to Christian Science* (New York: University Books).

counter-allegations, movements within the political and religious life of their times, combined to create a tangled web with many reputations at stake.

Secondly, while much of the debate about the legitimacy of hypnosis appeared to be undertaken within the framework of scientific observation and legal process, there was also a good deal of allegation and reporting which relied on conjecture and inference. Unsubstantiated fears grew, more based on warnings of dangers, stories of abuses, and threats to individual persons and society as a whole than on documented evidence. This point is of particular significance today, since many of the fears and cautions expressed in our time have their origins in those early days, based on evidence as flimsy as ever. These broad propositions will now be pursued in a little more detail, though for the serious scholar other more detailed accounts are recommended.[3]

Mesmer and animal magnetism

Anton Mesmer's personal background provides an interesting mix of the elements of the tensions noted above. Born in Austria, he initially decided on becoming a Jesuit priest, but, after four years of study, changed his direction due to a scientific interest in astronomy which he pursued for a while, attending law school for one year before he settled down to study medicine. He graduated as a physician in 1766 with a thesis that investigated the influence of the planets on human diseases.

Some years later, around 1773, he met Father Maximilian Hell, a figure with whom he had a great deal in common, being a Jesuit priest involved in healing. Father Hell was exploring the use of magnets in treatment, and was investigating and using 'magnetic medicine' to treat nervous conditions, among others, shaping magnets to fit body parts. The use of magnets and electricity was becoming popular at this time. Mesmer, however, was not persuaded that the magnets themselves were critical to the healing process, and argued that the benefits were derived from a universal fluid present in the physician and the patient. He developed an elaborate system for linking patients together and enabling the transmission of the magnetic fluid which was believed to generate convulsive crises.

The following extract from an extended description of the 'baquet' developed by Mesmer and a colleague, Charles D'Elson, captures the atmosphere generated in their Paris clinic in the late 1770s:

---

[3] See especially Edmonston, W. E. (1986), *The induction of hypnosis* (New York: Wiley); Laurence & Perry, *Hypnosis, will and memory*.

> Fountains, an orchestra, well-designed gardens, four wooden tubs, or 'baquets,' and later on, a magnetized tree for the benefit of the poor, completed the arrangement . . . To better understand the atmosphere surrounding the new treatment, it is of interest to describe the baquet and what occurred around it. . . . Upon arrival at Mesmer's clinic patients were taken to a dimly lit room which was adorned with heavy drapes and zodiacal and masonic signs painted on the walls. The patients were asked to sit around a table that was the cover of a circular oak box, 18 inches high and 6 feet in diameter. This box, or tub, was the baquet. It contained water, broken glass and iron filings. Over these objects were placed symmetrical rows of bottles filled with water. In each row, the necks of the bottles alternately converged and diverged from the center of the box. It was believed that the more rows, the greater the curative power of the baquet. The water level was adjusted depending on the types of effects desired. The whole box was covered by a wooden panel which had a number of holes, through which either glass or iron rods protruded. Each rod was bent at an angle that allowed one extremity to be in water while the other could be applied to the patient's body. Since there were often many rows of patients around each baquet, the rods came in varying lengths.
>
> When everyone was in position, a rope was tied loosely around each person sitting at the baquet until it was returned to the tub. This rope provided two functions: First, it permitted the magnetic fluid to circulate through everybody before being redirected into the baquet . . . Second, it was through this rope that the magnetist induced the movement of the magnetic fluid. In order to be effective, the magnetist had to be part of the chain. Once the magnetist had roped the people together, it was thought that nothing could prevent the dissemination of the magnetic fluid.[4]

The intention of this approach was to bring about dramatic convulsions in those who were sick, in the belief that they would then be cured. Such reactions were achieved in about a quarter of those who participated. Mesmer, dressed flamboyantly, conducted the proceedings rather like an orchestra, as Laurence and Perry put it.

While Mesmer had challenged the need of magnets in producing powerful reactions, he had generated his own theory of fluids, and developed paraphernalia to bring about results which were themselves challenged by the medical profession. He was accused of immoral behaviour with some patients and his theory became the subject of enquiries, as a result of which the animal magnetism explanation fell into disrepute. Nonetheless, even among those who dismissed his explanations, there was wide recognition that powerful changes were induced, and some were ready to attribute these changes to the power of suggestion and the use of the patients' imagination.

---

[4] See Laurence & Perry, *Hypnosis, will and memory*, pp. 57–8

Recovering from Mesmer

The nineteenth century saw a gradual rehabilitation of what we have since come to call hypnosis. As mesmerism faded into disrepute, based on incorrect explanations, others recognized that the actual phenomena themselves might still have real value. For this shift, we have a neurologist and a surgeon to thank in particular. Jean-Martin Charcot (1835–1893) was a Parisian neurologist and director of the famous Salpetrière Hospital. He conceived hypnosis to be a neuropathological state, and linked this to views about dissociation in hysteria. This teaching was foundational to Sigmund Freud, one of Charcot's students, who went on to expound the theory of the unconscious. Hypnosis as a means used to explore hidden memories was the first tool of psychoanalysis, until it was replaced by Freud's 'free association' technique. Concurrently, in Britain, James Braid (1795–1860) was impressed by the medical possibilities of hypnosis. He considered the state to be a kind of sleep and hence coined the still confusing term 'hypnotism'. He was particularly struck by the observation of post-hypnotic amnesia, in which people later can forget what had happened in trance, and considered this a true hallmark of hypnosis. While Braid was interested in establishing a sound scientific basis for hypnotism, another British surgeon, James Esdaile, was achieving remarkable success in India with hypnotism as the sole anaesthetic in major procedures. His results were so impressive that colleagues sought to dismiss them as unfounded. Esdaile might have achieved greater fame if chemical anaesthesia had not developed at the same time, making the dramatic pain control achieved through hypnosis less necessary. So too, back in France, hypnosis might have achieved greater acceptance among psychotherapists had Freud not had such negative experiences with it. He is reported not to have been good at hypnosis himself, and after some difficulties declared it 'a failure and a method of doubtful ethical value'.[5] At the turn of the twentieth century Freud also began to separate from, and lose respect for, his mentor Pierre Janet. As Freud's reputation increased, Janet's decreased, and with it his advocacy of hypnosis; 'hypnosis was largely forsaken for treatment of the fully awake patient on the couch'.[6] So there came another decline in the acceptance of hypnosis, both for psychotherapy and for surgery. With

---

5 Ellenberger, H. F. (1970), *The discovery of the unconscious: The history and evolution of dynamic psychiatry* (New York: Basic Books), p.802.

6 North, C. S., Ryall, J. E. M., Ricci, D. A. & Wetzel, R. D. (1993), *Multiple personalities, multiple disorders* (New York: Oxford University Press), p. 10.

the need for anaesthesia met more simply by chemical means, many years were to pass before hypnosis would again achieve validity as a form of pain control, especially in dentistry and in the management of chronic pain. The ascendancy of psychoanalysis meant that hypnosis was not favoured, in deference to Freud's opinions, while in other areas of psychological therapy the emergence of behaviourism, with J. B. Watson and B. F. Skinner developing theories based on learning, left little place for any phenomena which could not be observed and measured. Hypnosis clearly did not fit into the world of behaviourism.

The professional rehabilitation of hypnosis has come as behaviourism has been found inadequate, and the recognition of cognitive processes has revived. It is now possible to blend the new understandings of behaviour, emotions and thoughts with the techniques of hypnosis to provide effective therapy. How long this resurgence will last remains to be seen. Foolishly ambitious claims for its use or disreputable abuse of its potential could plunge it once again into disfavour.

Science versus religion

This historical sequence illustrates the tensions that exist between the claims of the church and the claims of science. Mesmer himself moved from his commitment to training for priesthood across to a scientific training. Medicine was undergoing a transition away from treatments based on folklore and herbal remedies towards a more empirical basis, shaped by observation and experimentation. The theatrical nature of Mesmer's interventions was not welcomed by the professions generally, and his theories were open to careful scrutiny. Whereas, previously, it would have been the Catholic Church which would have issued statements based on investigation, the major impact at this time came from a series of inquiries from bodies such as the Royal Society of Medicine, and the Benjamin Franklin Commission ordered by King Louis XVI which also included medical practitioners.

The issue was not whether changes occurred, but what the explanation for these might be. As no claims were made of demonic possession, this was no longer the province of the church. The issue was one of the legitimacy of animal magnetism as a form of medical practice. The commissions concluded in 1784, by the use of both observation and experiments, that Mesmer's explanations were incorrect. While the Royal Commission declared the approach dangerous, especially to morality, the medical community doubted its therapeutic efficacy and required physicians to sign that they would not practise animal magnetism.

This period of intense investigation and enquiry effectively ended the era of animal magnetism and mesmerism, although Mesmer himself lived until 1815. Up to this point it appeared that therapeutic benefits were usually, though not exclusively, the product of the dramatic crises attributed to magnetic effects. While the emphasis on theatrical and spectacular responses lives on in stage hypnosis, the trend in clinical work has been quite the reverse. This shift is directly attributable to the work of one of Mesmer's disciples, the Marquis de Puysegur, who happened upon what he called 'somnambulistic sleep'.

While still retaining some of Mesmer's procedures (using a tree as his baquet) he found eventually that not only was touching unnecessary, but good results came also from a deep sleep-like experience. Hence, it became possible to conceive that the relationship was important (what we would now call a good rapport), and that patients were actually able to achieve a good deal of what they needed through their own insights. He provided a basis for many of the contemporary assumptions of clinical hypnosis, while others took his ideas into the world of spiritualism, to utilize what appeared to be clairvoyance and telepathy.

The Catholic Church and possession

A contemporary of Anton Mesmer was Johann Gassner, a Catholic priest who experienced symptoms which he attributed to possession. Following a successful exorcism, he developed his own skills as an exorcist for those suffering from conditions attributed to the devil. He used techniques which are comparable to those used by the Church in earlier days for identifying witches, and which bear comparison with contemporary stage hypnosis. He attracted the attention of the Church as a result of his claims to be an exorcist and was asked to retire to a community. He also attracted the attention of the state, in that the Prince Elector Max-Joseph of Bavaria established a commission which invited evidence from Mesmer.

Laurence and Perry[7] describe the circumstances surrounding Gassner, indicating the parallels between his techniques and those of hypnosis:

> Mesmer . . . demonstrated that all of Gassner's effects could be reproduced without

---

7 Laurence & Perry, *Hypnosis, will and memory*, pp. 5–9.

> recourse to the rituals of exorcism. Initially, he explained that the priest was in reality only acting on the patient's imagination . . . It is also important to recognize that in the exorcism of Emilie, one can find many of the major behaviors and subjective experiences that were later to be associated with hypnosis in the nineteenth century as well as most of the hypnotic behaviors investigated by contemporary researchers. These include rigidity of the body or specific body parts, the manipulation of pain perception, and suggested hallucinations of deafness and blindness.[8]

Laurence and Perry note how easy it is to misread an apparent indicator of demonic possession in that the subject Emilie was shown to respond to a Latin command after a discourse in French. Although Gassner made no mention of it, Emilie apparently already understood Latin due to her education.[9] Another feature often linked to possession is the presentation of an involuntary state of 'being possessed' and seemingly lacking in personal control over behaviour. In contemporary hypnotic techniques, dissociation of parts is readily achieved by depersonalized communication. So, for example, instead of giving an instruction, 'I want you to lift your arm', the command 'The arm will now lift' results in the subject having a strong sense of a response not under voluntary control. It is not difficult then to infer, where possession is suspected, that a demonic presence has produced the resulting arm levitation. Laurence and Perry comment that, 'During the exorcism Gassner did not command Emilie directly, but rather addressed himself to the evil force inside her. This semantic sophistication helped to create the experience of an involuntary possession state.'[10]

These events were significant, then, in making a major transition from predominantly religious interpretations of involuntary behaviour to the use of science and reason, based on experimentation. It was a time of ambivalence within the Church as the conventional teachings of Catholicism came under scrutiny. There was similar ambivalence in the scientific community as practices which claimed to be scientific were investigated and found to be unsubstantiated. Neither religion nor science could claim to have triumphed over the other, nor was either party totally discredited. Rather, it became possible to be more discerning when questions of possession were raised, while the use of hypnotic techniques moved from false theoretical foundations towards a period of intense scientific scrutiny. Neither process has yet been completed as we still lack adequate explanations for hypnotic phenomena, and the issue of demon possession is

---

8 ibid. p. 7.
9 ibid.
10 ibid. p. 9, and see full transcript, pp. 19–21.

one of revived interest and great contention. The tension between models of intervention is further explored below.

Orthodoxy and heterodoxy

The scientific developments of the eighteenth and nineteenth centuries challenged traditional religious views of the demonic and the nature of exorcisms, but a strong spiritual tradition remained. From a Christian perspective, the spiritual interpretation of phenomena has gone two ways. Within mainstream Christian thinking the possibility of spiritual influence on a person's life has remained, with attributions being made to the influence of both God and the devil in human affairs. Although there have been pressures within the liberal churches to discard a personal devil, and largely discount the significance of sin, this trend runs the risk, by its own logic, of concluding that if there is no evil then there can be no good; if there is no devil, then maybe God does not exist either. It is a short step to a crisis of faith and the development of a secular humanistic view of the world.

Orthodox Christian thinking still claims the presence of both good and evil, God and the devil, together with a personal responsibility for one's actions. Within that framework the existence of evil[11] and its active presence in the world continues to be taken seriously, along with the power of God to triumph over evil. Responses to this by Christians vary widely, some relying on evangelism to achieve personal conversion to faith, others looking to change the evils of society collectively, and yet others seeking to engage in direct confrontations with demonic presences either through exorcisms or inner healing ministries. The healing role of the church, while modified by the growth of secular healing professions, remains viable today, continuing to claim impressive results. There remains a serious responsibility to ensure that interventions directed against evil, and claiming spiritual power, do in fact derive their effectiveness in this way, and do not simply repeat the misguided excesses of the past. It is at this point that the use of hypnosis may be perceived as a challenge to spiritual approaches – claiming similar effects without invoking the power of God – or as a powerful explanatory principle, helping us to see how things happen the way they do. I prefer the second option as a means of bridging the secular and spiritual areas of discourse.

---

[11] Including Scott Peck, M. (1983), *People of the Lie* (New York: Simon and Schuster).

There was a period of quite intense confrontation of traditional evangelistic approaches with hypnosis (or mesmerism) in the years following 1830 in America. During the period following the Second Great Awakening, a time of intense spiritual revival in America, mesmerism was being presented as a kind of alternative spiritual answer to human need. This historical development has been carefully documented by Richard Fuller who says: 'Like the revivalists before them, the mesmerists preached that confusion, self-doubt, and demoralization would continue to plague the people as long as they refused to open themselves up to a higher spiritual power. Mesmerism, no less than revivalism, provided confused individuals with an intense experience thought to bring them into inner harmony with unseen spiritual forces.'[12]

At the same time, hypnotic techniques have also led others into heterodoxy. Developments in spiritualism and in Christian Science have undoubtedly built on phenomena observed during the days of Mesmer and de Puysegur.[13] As the latter developed his understanding of somnambulistic sleep, for example, it became evident that the 'subject appeared to become clairvoyant when in such a sleep which allowed him or her to know how to behave in artificial somnambulism and how to instruct the magnetist. The patient also appeared to become telepathic and seemed to know the unspoken thoughts of his or her magnetist.'[14] De Puysegur himself went on to develop the possibilities of this approach by forming the Society of Universal Harmony in France.

In America, we are told by Kelly, an initial proponent of mesmerism named Andrew Jackson Davis began leading supporters of mesmerism into the new faith of spiritualism. At about the same time, mesmerism was developed into a new healing system by Phineas Parkhurst Quimby (1802–66), a professional mesmerist who felt that many diseases could be cured by suggestion and were therefore essentially illusory. Eventually drawing the conclusion that all diseases are illusory, Quimby in 1859 began teaching the system he called Science of Christ, Science of Health, and occasionally Christian Science. His system later developed into the New Thought movement and, led by Mary Baker Eddy who began her career as a mesmerist and a spiritualist medium, into Christian Science.[15]

---

12 Fuller, *Mesmerism and the American cure of souls*, pp. 78–9.
13 Podmore, *From Mesmer to Christian Science.*
14 Laurence and Perry, *Hypnosis, will and memory*, p. 108.
15 Kelly, 'Hypnosis and self-hypnosis', pp.229–30.

Although Kelly identifies this development as being associated with mesmerism, this does not altogether do justice to Quimby's own approach since, although he started out as a mesmerist and believed animal magnetism to be the source of influence, he eventually discarded that interpretation in favour of a belief that powerful positive suggestion was the mediating influence.[16] The endorsement by Mary Baker Eddy of hypnosis (and her later disavowal of it) created a climate within which orthodox Christians eschewed the same phenomena as too closely linked to false teaching.[17]

In the more recent past, hypnotic techniques have been readily embraced by the New Age movement, which has emphasized the value of meditation for self-discovery, and visualization for such purposes as achieving health and discerning life-goals. This contemporary religious expression places responsibility and choice clearly within the individual, and makes no attribution to a personal God or devil.[18]

With hypnosis so widely incorporated by many religious groups in our Western culture, we should not be surprised that it features strongly in the religious practices of many other cultural and religious groups. Traditional religious healers use not only the naturally occurring physical resources such as herbs to bring relief, but also draw on the interpersonal influence of techniques based on suggestion and influence. Indeed, in a worldwide survey, covering 488 societies, it was found that 89 per cent displayed socially approved ASCs, described by a wide variety of terms.[19] Within their use for healing purposes, there appear to be four main groupings of practitioners – shamans, priests and priestesses, mediums and diviners, and malevolent practitioners.[20] They all use ASCs and, while in the Western scientific tradition these practices might be described as hypnotic in their character, this is no more accurate than describing them as variations of inner healing or deliverance ministries.

Behind the common themes it is important to acknowledge that the varied uses of ASCs derive their special characteristics from cultural and

---

16 Morton, *Hypnosis and pastoral counseling*, p. 61.

17 For a more extended account of the relationship between Quimby, Christian Science and hypnosis, see Podmore, *From Mesmer to Christian Science* and Anderson, *C. A. (1993) Healing hypotheses* (New York: Garland Publishing).

18 See Kelly, 'Hypnosis and self-hypnosis', p. 228.

19 Bourgignon, E. & Evascus, T. (1977), 'Altered states of consciousness within a general evolutionary perspective: A holocultural analysis', *Behavioral Science Research, 12*, 199–216.

20 This analysis based on 47 traditional societies by Winkelmann, M. (1984), 'A cross-cultural study of magico-religious practitioners' in Heinze, R. I. (ed), *Proceedings of the International Conference on Shamanism* (Berkeley, CA: Independent Scholars of Asia).

religious assumptions about the source of healing and the ways in which sickness is understood. In theistic cultures the attribution of effectiveness is to the deity, whereas others look within for the healing powers. Sickness is variously explained as related to the will of the gods, or to links with ancestors, to personal behaviour, or to environmental factors. Even in our own society we have various ways of attributing illness, incorporating all of these possibilities. What one calls the judgment of God will be attributed to demonic influence by another; a third may look to the dysfunctional family or the influence of past generations as yet unresolved; a fourth may favour an explanation in terms of choices the individual has made; a fifth may look to the inner environment of genetic difference or physical differences, or maybe to the outer environment of a world full of hazards. Some of these attributions may carry strong Christian assumptions, while others have little relationship at all to religious explanations of any kind. If this is so with the sicknesses people experience, so too with the means they choose to achieve healing. Our society, as with others, prefers some explanations over others and adopts healing strategies consistent with them.

In a cross-cultural discussion of hypnosis, with particular attention to Native American practices, Stanley Krippner develops both the similarities and differences of many healing traditions, and notes:

> The ubiquitous nature of hypnotic-like procedures in native healing is also the result of the ways in which human capacities – such as the capability to strive toward a goal and the ability to imagine a suggested experience – can be channeled and shaped, albeit differentially, by social interaction. Concepts of sickness and healing can be socially constructed and modeled in a number of ways. The models found in traditional cultures frequently identify such etiological factors in sickness as 'soul loss', 'breach of taboo', or 'spirit possession', 'intrusion' or 'invasion' – all of which are diagnosed (at least in part) by observable changes in the victims' behavior as related to their mentation and mood.[21]

The conventional explanations offered by Western psychiatry have largely disregarded such concepts, preferring to identify anything religious as pathological, though this pattern is now changing to a more balanced recognition of the authenticity of religious experience.[22] At the same time,

---

[21] Krippner, S. (1993), 'Cross cultural perspectives on hypnotic-like procedures used by native healing practitioners', in Rhue, Lynn & Kirsch, *Handbook of clinical hypnosis*, pp. 692–3.

[22] See e.g., Larson, D. B. *et al.* (1986), 'Systematic analysis of research on religious variables in four major psychiatric journals, 1978–1982' *American Journal of Psychiatry, 143*, 3, 329–34; and a substantial review article by Worthington, E. V., Jr., Kurusu, T. A., McCullough, M. E. & Sandage, S. J. (1996), 'Empirical research on religion and psychotherapeutic processes and outcomes: A 10-year review and research prospectus', *Psychological Bulletin, 119*, 3, 448–87.

the Christian church has retained explanations of this kind, in terms such as possession, demonization, and infestation by evil spirits. If we assume that such concepts have any validity at all, we cannot at the same time disregard these other religious explanations or the means used to bring relief. What we may do is to discern those modes of healing which can be authentically embraced within Christian theology in that they emanate from a Christian worldview and/or are not inconsistent with it.

The truth is that significant healing is achieved by practitioners from vastly different traditions. While some appeal to demons, some to other gods, others to the Holy Spirit, and yet others to science, 'successful' outcomes are claimed by all. While we can legitimately claim that all healing ultimately derives from God, not all practitioners or sufferers acknowledge this, and Krippner draws our attention to this by saying,

> Torrey (1986) surveyed indigenous psychotherapists, concluding (on the basis of anecdotal reports) that 'many of them are effective psychotherapists and produce therapeutic change in their clients.' Torrey observed that when the effectiveness of psychotherapy paraprofessionals has been studied, professionals have not been found to demonstrate superior skills. The sources of that effectiveness are the four basic components of psychotherapy: A shared world view, personal qualities of the healer, client expectations, and a process that enhances the client's learning and mastery. Strupp (1972) added, 'The modern psychotherapist . . . relies to a large extent on the same psychological mechanisms used by the faith healer, shaman, physician, priest, and others, and the results, as reflected by the evidence of therapeutic outcomes appear to be substantially similar.'[23]

It would appear to be a desire to preserve orthodoxy against dangerous intrusions that led Ellen White to direct those in the Seventh Day Adventist tradition to guard against hypnosis, and such cautions remain deeply entrenched today. Writing in the nineteenth century she warned against mesmerism, since that was the contemporary term, and bracketed it with phrenology and spiritualism. In a reconsideration of the Seventh Day Adventist changed position, Berecz indicates that Ellen White was dealing with her own concerns lest her visionary experiences, attributed by herself to an encounter with God, might be dismissed as arising from mesmerism. She also expressed the fear that those who used mesmerism might succumb to pride, and attribute any successes to personal influence rather than the power of God.[24]

Although her injunctions have been taken by many as absolutely rejecting the practice of hypnosis, Berecz has noted that she is actually

---

23 'Cross cultural perspectives', pp. 711–12.

24 Berecz, 'Hypnosis – Yes: SDAs should use it', p. 3.

more balanced in her position: 'Phrenology and mesmerism are very much exalted. They are good in their place, but are seized upon by Satan as his most powerful agents to deceive and destroy souls.'[25] The pros and cons of the case have been presented for Seventh Day Adventists in *Spectrum*, an Adventist journal, in which Berecz argues as a clinical psychology professor for the legitimacy of hypnosis in therapy, while a contrary view is provided by an ethicist, Provonsha, under the title 'Hypnosis – No: it may be a sin'.[26] In his rebuttal Provonsha employs many of the stereotypical views of hypnosis addressed in various parts of this book, and especially the spectre of dehumanizing manipulation, to argue his case. In that issue of *Spectrum* a final article by Mastrapa speaks very positively of the value of hypnosis in the context of prayer and meditation.[27]

Together, these writers point to the need to separate the wheat from the chaff, to recognize that incidental evil (from abuse of the technique) is different from intrinsic evil (which would warrant rejection of the technique altogether). Disagreements continue as assorted phenomena are brought together and treated as if they were all the same, and fixed positions are adopted through quotation and misquotation of authors instead of study of the available evidence.

Who are the healers?

The discussion of alternative approaches to healing invites the more general question about who is to be considered in a society as a legitimate healer, and who is marginal or even disapproved. That struggle for authenticity has been most obvious in the West as the long-standing hegemony of the church as the natural location of healing was eroded by the development of modern medicine with its scientific paradigm largely replacing the earlier assumptions that linked sickness to sin and the disfavour of God. Although the church played an active part, especially in Europe, in the establishment of hospitals, the specifically spiritual element in healing has been greatly reduced both for physical and mental health conditions.

In our society the medical community is undoubtedly seen as the primary vehicle for healing and this is enshrined in the way health, and

---

[25] Quoted in ibid. p. 36.

[26] Provonsha, J. (1994), 'Hypnosis – No: It may be a sin', *Spectrum*, *23*, 4, 42–8.

[27] Mastrapa, S. C. (1994), 'Hypnosis – Maybe: If it's like prayer', *Spectrum*, *23*, 4, 49–50.

payment for health services, is controlled substantially by the medical profession. Other groups have varying degrees of legitimacy in their respective fields and can claim independent expertise, but always in relation to where medicine stands. Hypnosis as a practice has commonly found itself on the fringe not only because it lacks the scientific foundations of physical sciences, but because it is practised predominantly by psychologists and other therapists who are often viewed as adjunctive to medicine. Those who offer spiritual healing, or work in healing ministries, are usually even further from the centre, being seen as interesting variants or last resorts when other approaches have failed. This does not necessarily represent a lack of effectiveness or competence, but does indicate that the predominating world view is scientific rather than religious.

In primitive or native cultures, it can be difficult to persuade a sufferer to go to a Western physician rather than the witch-doctor, because their world view gives legitimacy to the local form of healing. The exact opposite applies in Western culture where the medical approach is presumed to be normative. The bi-cultural Chinese living in the West can choose between the healing traditions of the East (herbal remedies, acupuncture, etc.) and those of the West, recognizing that their underlying assumptions about cause and cure are very different.

Within the ebb and flow of legitimate healing approaches, hypnosis has had a chequered career, moving between faddish enthusiasm and public disapproval. The wave of enthusiasm initially engendered by Mesmer in the eighteenth century was followed by a period of disfavour following the enquiries which showed his assumptions to be ill-founded. In the nineteenth century a resurgence of interest might have become greater in the days of Freud and Janet as they explored the possibilities of hypnosis for the treatment of dissociative disorders, and for its anaesthetic possibilities for surgery. However, the development of chemical anaesthesia forestalled the latter, while Freud's problems with, and rejection of, hypnosis contributed to its decline as a tool in psychotherapy.

This period of decline in scientific acceptance has gradually reversed over the last forty to fifty years, while the vogue for Freudian psychoanalysis has been waning. The therapeutic practice of hypnosis is thoroughly endorsed and widely used in the medical, dental and psychological professions, no longer as a somewhat mystical and questionable activity, but increasingly based on solidly researched foundations. Even though it remains difficult to understand exactly what hypnosis is, there is no doubt that it is a powerful tool when used by competently trained practitioners. Just as the professionals were slow to acknowledge the therapeutic respectability of hypnosis, in view of its dubious history, so too many in the churches retain long-standing fears, not yet ready to embrace that which is helpful for fear of that which might be harmful.

In view of the remarkable similarity between hypnosis and spiritual healing techniques – in many ways a link which is a good deal closer than hypnosis can claim to the scientific traditions of medicine – one might have expected more hostility from science and less from religion. However, when we ask who are the legitimately recognized healers, it becomes clear that, while medicine has nothing to lose by incorporating hypnotic techniques along with others, Christian healers often seek to establish an authentic and independant claim to healing. In endorsing a spiritual model to explain what happens, hypnosis can make uncomfortable claims to be doing things similar to what Christian healers claim, but without invoking a spiritual explanation. Hence, we would expect hypnosis to be criticized and rejected as unspiritual and unbiblical, to be avoided, by those who look to the power of God for healing.

If, indeed, there is some foundation to the accusation that hypnosis is secular whereas inner healing approaches are truly spiritual, then a warning to Christians is in order. If the accusation is taken still further to say that hypnosis is not merely secular but also forbidden in Scripture as inevitably a part of occult practices, then the case against hypnosis is even stronger. The objections from Scripture are discussed elsewhere (see Chapters 2 and 8). The objection that hypnosis is secular and not spiritual is of a different order. This would suggest two things: Firstly, it suggests that 'spiritual' interventions are always better than 'secular' ones. This proposition is only convincing if we insist on separating the world in that way. Most Christians will argue that 'secular' medicine is actually under the ultimate rule of God, who is the Healer, whether the physician recognizes this or not. This same concept also undergirds the work of many therapists in the mental health area – that therapy should be conducted competently, whoever the therapist may be, and the Christian is one who gives God the glory when healing occurs. Under these circumstances, skilled intervention can be more healing than prayer offered by one who fails to recognize the real nature of the problem. Those who resort to casting out demons when no demons are present can do more harm than good, setting healing back and leaving people rather the worse. Secondly, in considering secular versus spiritual, we should also recognize that at the heart of such dissent is the goal which is intended for healing. The truth is that if we ask the spiritual healer to define the purpose of such healing, it will be expressed in spiritual terms.

It may be to bring out an improved relationship with God, or freedom from oppression, or dealing with chronic blocks to spiritual maturity. While these are all legitimate spiritual outcomes, they represent a different agenda from that of the typical mental health professional. Therapy, including the use of hypnosis, is used to bring about change in adjustment, in coping strategies, in personal relationships and in dealing with past hurts. The professional therapist who is a Christian is paid to work on the latter. At the same time, their world view is such that the spiritual dimensions of many problems are also recognized and can be addressed. It is not necessary to separate out these areas of needs and there is evidence to indicate that when psychological issues are addressed by those who share the same world view, outcomes are more likely to be favourable.[28] When we acknowledge that the focus of activity is different, then the need to compete for legitimacy evaporates. Instead, there can develop a mutual respect and a willingness to refer to one another according to the perceived focus of issues needing attention.

Unfortunately that apparent dichotomy into spiritual matters and secular ones, as if they were different in kind and can be recognized as such, is too simplistic. It was the essence of the first concern above that we really cannot separate secular and spiritual so neatly. Even though we may for convenience refer to categories such as body, mind, and spirit, such sub-divisions are neither truly biblical nor able to do justice to the holistic integration of functioning by which we are all of these all the time. Hence, if I, as a therapist, want to argue that I am seeking to offer treatment for depression, and this is a psychological matter, I can expect an immediate challenge from the physician who emphasizes a biological component which may respond to medication. At the same time, the case for addressing depression as a spiritual matter can also be made, as well as approaches to healing which use spiritual resources.

This kind of overlap is the rule rather than the exception, so there is little hope that the various healing groups can agree to occupy different territories and cross-refer with mutual recognition. Problems needing resolution will be defined according to who is approached for help. Those who first consult their doctor invariably report symptoms

---

[28] Bergin, A. E. (1980), 'Psychotherapy and religious values', *Journal of Consulting and Clinical Psychology*, *48*, 1, 95–105. Tan, S. Y. (1993). 'Training in professional psychology: Diversity includes religion', in *Clinical Training in Professional Psychology*, National Council of Schools of Professional Psychology Conference Proceedings, 1993, pp. 183–96. Worthington, E. V., Jr. (ed), *Psychotherapy and religious values* (Grand Rapids, MI: Baker Book House).

they expect a doctor to recognize. Those who go first to their pastor may have the self-same problem, but will use very different language to describe it: the pastor will ask quite different questions by way of exploration, and propose a different remedy. So, too, the mental health professional will focus differently, relying on other models of understanding human behaviour to decide what is wrong and what should be done. If we are not so myopic as to believe that we, and we alone, have the answers, those who seek help will usually find their way to the approach most helpful to them. Prayerful discernment may identify a spiritual issue; it may also suggest a visit to the surgeon for a very different kind of help.

Church positions on hypnosis

Against such a background, some churches who take hypnosis seriously have found it necessary to declare their position regarding its use. The Roman Catholic Church, with its interest in physical as well as other forms of healing, has made various statements over the years, never condemning hypnosis outright but cautioning against its misuse. Even as far back as Mesmer's days of animal magnetism, a decree of 1847 stated that 'the use of animal magnetism is indeed merely an act making use of physical media that are otherwise licit and hence it is not morally forbidden, provided that it does not tend toward an illicit end or toward anything depraved'.[29]

A similar cautious endorsement was provided in statements by Pope Pius XII, published in 1956 and 1957.[30] The Catholic position today can therefore be summarized in three points:

(a) Hypnosis is a serious scientific matter, and not something to be dabbled in.
(b) In its scientific use the precautions dictated by both science and morality are to be heeded.
(c) In its use for anaesthesia it is governed by the same principle as any other form of anaesthesia.

---

[29] Collectanea Sanctae Congregationis de Propaganda Fide, No. 1018, editio anni: 1907, see Kroger, *Clinical and experimental hypnosis*, p. 127.

[30] See Venn, 'Hypnosis for Christians' Mangan, J. T. (1959), 'Hypnosis: A medico-moral evaluation', *Linacre Quarterly*, *26*, 39.

In a discussion of various religions in relation to hypnosis, Kroger describes not only the Roman Catholic position but also that of Judaism, finding a good deal of similarity between hypnosis and their religious practices.

> Prayer, particularly in the Jewish and Christian religions, has many similarities to hypnotic induction. There is the regular cadence and intonation in the prayers (chanting), a relaxing environment, and the fixation of attention on the altar or religious leader. In Judaism, there is the rhythmic rocking of the body back and forth in time to the chanting which is hypnagogic. Finally, the contemplation, the meditation and the self-absorption characteristic of prayer are almost identical with hypnosis.[31]

I had hoped to find some considered statement provided by mainstream Protestant churches, and evangelicals in particular, but in this I was unsuccessful. Certainly, there are a number of individuals who write about hypnosis, and indicate its clinical value, but it appears that the cautions typically voiced by Christians derive from either early Catholic teaching or from the work of Kurt Koch. It would be quite refreshing for practitioners to find church boards willing to examine the contemporary state of knowledge and to issue guiding statements. Such statements would also liberate many who seek help secretively because they are so unsure about where their church stands. Accumulating what little has been said by way of direction, there appears to be general support for hypnosis when practised ethically by trained professionals, with no indication that in such settings the risks are unacceptable. A useful summary along these lines is offered by Venn:

> Hypnosis is a normal, natural phenomenon the practice of which does not conflict with Christian belief as long as it remains within the ethical guidelines that pertain to all forms of psychological investigation and treatment . . . However, some hypnotists do conduct unethical or occult practices, and the public is advised to be cautious about whom they let hypnotize them and for what reason.[32]

---

[31] Kroger, 'Clinical and experimental hypnosis', p. 125.
[32] Venn, 'Hypnosis for Christians', p. 5.

Chapter 8

Challenging the Stereotypes

Differing Christian views of hypnosis

Not everyone thinks hypnosis is a good thing, even when it is applied clinically and with the best of intentions. The strongest objections come from Christians who argue that there is something fundamentally wrong with hypnosis. A good deal of this writing comes from the 1970s, and involves secondary reporting as much as personal opinion. In 1969 H. E. Freeman published *Angels of light?* which included a sweeping rejection of hypnosis in any form. In a strongly worded condemnation he wrote that, 'One of the most subtle and potentially dangerous forms of magical practice is hypnosis, an ancient occult method of influence or control of the mind and action of others. The greatest threat lies in the fact that in the hypnotized state of the surrendered will, the individual is open to the invasion of evil spirits.'[1] In 1971 Dennis and Rita Bennett followed in Freeman's footsteps, asserting that hypnosis can allow access to satanic forces and involves control of one person by another rather than by the Holy Spirit. 'Hypnosis, by placing the soul in a passively receptive state, opens the door to morbid spiritual influences . . .'[2]

Biblical support is offered for such views with reference to Deuteronomy 18:10–11 which deserves exact quotation since it appears to be the sole source advanced as a reference to hypnosis:

> There shall not be found among you anyone . . . who practises divination, a soothsayer, or an augur, or a sorcerer, or a charmer, or a medium, or a wizard, or a necromancer (*Revised Standard Version*).

In the *New International Version* this reads (my emphasis added):

---

1 Freeman, H. E. (1969), *Angels of light?* (Plainfield, NJ: Logos International), p. 56.
2 Bennett, D. & R. (1971), *The Holy Spirit and you* (Plainfield, NJ: Logos International).

> Let no one be found among you . . . who practises divination or sorcery, interprets omens, engages in witchcraft, or *casts spells*, or who is a medium or a spiritist or who consults the dead.

I have often asked students to guess which of those terms refer to hypnosis, yet, even when versed in Hebrew, they show a low success rate. Other modern translations provide no additional clues leading one to expect that 'charmers' are supposed to be synonymous with hypnotists. Reference back to the original Hebrew term in this text suggests it has to do with magic and sorcery, and is linked to idolatry. The *New Brown-Driver-Briggs-Gesenius Hebrew English Lexicon* offers several possibilities for the term used here, with the verb meaning to 'unite, be joined, tie a magic knot or spell, charm'. The Lexicon translates the verb to mean 'to join together; to bind, to fascinate, spoken of some kind of magic which was applied to the binding of magical knots; cf. German bannen=binden, and other words which signify binding, which are applied to incantations'.[3] It becomes even clearer when we find the same word in Psalm 58:5 referring unmistakably to snake-charming as part of occultic practice. 'Their venom is like the venom of a snake, like that of a cobra that has stopped its ears, that will not heed the time of the *charmer*, however skilful the enchanter may be' (NIV). The Gesenius lexicon cross-refers to this passage and understands the term to refer to 'the incantation of serpents'. The passage in Leviticus does not necessarily carry this implication, but appears to be a more general statement regarding the casting of spells and charms.

Since the exegesis of this verse is central to any Christian objection to hypnosis, I consulted Dr Fred Bush, the D. Wilson Moore Professor of Ancient New Eastern Studies at Fuller Theological Seminary, about these opinions. With his extensive background in and knowledge of Eastern languages, he agreed with the analysis I have offered here, and added: 'To use these passages as a reference to hypnosis is exegetically indefensible.'[4]

More pungently, R. B. Morton has expressed the opinion that,

> To find otherwise highly intelligent men speaking of the subject out of a warehouse of ignorance and in the authoritative manner is an inexcusable affront to integrity. Thousands of people have been influenced to disregard hypnosis as a viable therapeutic modality by such inaccurate and prejudiced writing. Hobart E. Freeman in his book *Angels of light?* includes all hypnosis (without exception) in those practices which are condemned by God. By quoting Deuteronomy 18:9ff

---

[3] *New Brown-Driver-Briggs-Gesenius Hebrew and English Lexicon* (1951) (Oxford: Clarendon Press), p. 288.

[4] Personal communication, 1994.

> and interpreting hypnosis as being the act of 'charming,' the author indicates his lack of exegetical accuracy, and his prejudice towards a subject he has not fully investigated.[5]

Nonetheless, Freeman's view remains widely quoted[6] and has been influential in some Christian circles. Much the same position has been advanced by Bob Larson in a provocatively titled work, *Acupuncture: The hypnotic and the demonic*, in which he proposes a definition, 'Hypnosis is a state of hyper-suggestibility whereby the conscious control of one's mind and will is surrendered to the hypnotist.'[7] While hyper-suggestibility is correctly identified, the view that one's mind and will are surrendered to another rests on an obsolete and inadequate understanding of hypnosis. From that inadequate statement, the rest of Larson's caution follows naturally: 'no Christian should ever practice or submit to hypnosis . . . Allowing another to usurp control of one's will places the person hypnotized into a state of vulnerability to the invasion of evil spirits.'[8]

This type of 'surrender' is *not* characteristic of the therapeutic use of hypnosis. It is arguably true of stage hypnosis, and of many forms of hypnotic-like ASCs seen in religious practices. As practised by ethical practitioners today, hypnosis is associated with a high level of cooperation, agreement, and mutuality. The distinction between types of hypnosis and their uses is made more carefully by the missionary writer Kurt Koch whose caution, based on extensive observation of occultic practices in Asia, have been a widely quoted source of concern.[9] Indeed, he provides a sound basis for saying that hypnosis *can be* associated with the occult, and that the risk of openness to the demonic is legitimate. There is extensive and undisputed evidence that ASCs and religious practices are intimately related, so it follows that occultic practices and ASCs can occur together.[10] An objection to hypnosis *per se* on such grounds is an error of reasoning, since it confuses the practice of hypnosis with the purpose for which it is used. In fact, although Koch is ostensibly the Christian authority regarding the occultic dangers of hypnosis, he is careful to make the distinction between practice and purpose. Having identified the dangers of hypnosis used in occultic settings he then adds: 'The medical

---

[5] Morton, *Hypnosis and pastoral counseling*, p. 3.
[6] See e.g. Otis, G. K. (1973), *Like a roaring lion* (Van Nuys: Time Light).
[7] Larson, R. (1975), *Acupuncture: The hypnotic and the demonic* (Denver, CO: Bob Larson).
[8] ibid. p. 20.
[9] Koch, *Christian counseling and occultism.*
[10] Kroger, *Clinical and experimental hypnosis Ch. 25.*

profession uses hypnosis for diagnosis and therapy . . . Our concern is not with the professional use of hypnosis. Our main aim is to show by means of a few examples the dangers involved when hypnosis and suggestion are used by magic charmers and unqualified practitioners.'[11]

Clearly there is here a recognition that hypnosis can have value in professional settings. This more balanced appraisal has been followed by the authors of *Understanding the Occult*, who rely heavily on Koch's writings and summarize their position saying, 'Since there are so many examples of hypnosis which have ended in disaster, we would strongly warn people to stay away from all forms of either occultic or entertaining hypnosis. If a person allows himself to be hypnotized, it should be only under the most controlled situation by a qualified and experienced physician.'[12]

Unhappily, such statements have not settled the matter in all quarters. More recently there has been a strong surge of interest in deliverance ministries within the Pentecostal and charismatic parts of the church. The development of power evangelism and inner healing has been characterized by many remarkable examples of healing, physical and psychological as well as spiritual. In this context, it is not surprising that once again questions should be asked about the relationship of such signs and wonders to the claims of hypnosis. Are they similar? Are they the same thing, expressed in different terms? Are they antithetical to one another?

Current teaching on these matters is offered by John and Mark Sandford in their *Comprehensive guide to deliverance and inner healing.*[13] This ambitiously titled book gives a carefully constructed account of the experiences of the two authors in the development of their understanding of spiritual healing interventions. They reject the term 'inner healing' as a misnomer, commenting that 'Healing suggests fixing something that is broken, whereas God has no intention of fixing our soul.'[14] They propose that inner healing is actually evangelism.

This approach appears to be distinguishing a spiritual intervention from the work of therapists who seek to offer psychological care and might identify that there are some who need spiritual help and others who need psychological help. Unfortunately, after challenging the concept and arguing that inner healing is more than healing of memories or damaged

---

11 Koch, K. (n.d.), *The devil's alphabet* (W. Germany: Evangelistic Publishers), p. 71.

12 McDowell, J. & Stewart, D. (1982), *Understanding the occult* (San Bernardino, CA: Here's Life Publisher).

13 Grand Rapids, MI: Chosen books, 1992.

14 ibid. p. 53.

15 ibid. p. 165.

emotions, the Sandfords proceed to affirm that inner healing can be very effective with multiple personality disorder.[15] This psychiatric term, which has been intimately associated with hypnosis from its inception,[16] refers to a disorder where psychological healing is called for at all times, even if there are occasions when demonic elements are also present. Here Mark Sandford makes clear distinctions between the need to bring wholeness to the disintegrated parts, and the need to be sensitive to the possibility of the need for deliverance from evil.[17]

In spite of this acknowledgement of psychiatric issues and the importance of selecting a therapeutic approach which will not harm sufferers, the Sandfords include a section spelling out once again the traditional Christian objections to hypnosis. These demand careful consideration as we seek to understand what hypnosis is (and what it is not), since many readers of books such as the *Comprehensive guide* will base their beliefs on such assertions.

The Sandfords first trace contemporary hypnosis back to the work of Anton Mesmer, whose activities in the eighteenth century are discussed more fully in Chapter 7 below, where his errors are noted. They refer to the practice by the obsolete term 'hypnotism', which has been long abandoned in favour of hypnosis. The use of that term tends to cast doubt on hypnosis by suggesting an 'ism', a practice of dubious quality. They resurrect the objection to hypnosis that, among the occult practices listed in Deuteronomy 18, is 'one who casts a spell', and they state categorically: 'In biblical days hypnosis was spoken of as casting a spell, and a hypnotist was called a charmer.'[18] No support for this interpretation is offered, yet it is the only fundamental objection raised to hypnosis. If this question of definition is incorrect, then all the practical objections they raise after this are merely degrees of concern over misuse.

The last fifteen years have generally seen a more favourable attitude to hypnosis among Christian writers. One notable exception to this development toward a fuller understanding of the balance between benefits and hazards was the appearance in 1984 of a widely influential booklet

---

16 North, Ryall, Ricci & Wetzel, *Multiple personalities, multiple disorders.*

17 The term 'multiple personality disorder' is used here as the term which was in use until 1994, when the *Diagnostic and Statistical Manual (DSM IV)* introduced the more helpful diagnosis of Dissociative Identity Disorder (DID). This reformulation overcomes the philosophical problem of identifying many personalities in favour of recognizing one personality which has suffered fragmentation through dissociation.

18 Sandford, *Comprehensive guide to deliverance and inner healing*, pp. 328–9

19 Bobgan, *Hypnosis and the Christian.*

by Martin and Deirdre Bobgan entitled *Hypnosis and the Christian.*[19] Since this publication incorporates at some length many of the stereotypical dangers that were widely believed up to the 1970s, and which still linger today, I will explore their position more fully than others.

These two Christian writers, who have a background in psychology, engaged in a swingeing attack on hypnosis in all its expressions. Their writing provides an excellent example of the polarity of thinking which can emerge on a subject of importance even among those who come from similar biblical traditions. They address the same issues addressed in this book, and do so from an appraisal of the literature available to them at the time of their writing. They readily acknowledge and fully convey that there are Christians who favour the use of hypnosis, and represent why this is so. Yet in conclusion, when they have gone over similar ground to the material in this book, they come to a strikingly different conclusion, namely that 'Hypnotism is demonic at its worst and potentially damaging at its best.'[20] This conclusion was predictable in light of their earlier attacks on psychology presented as a tragic alternative to the Christian faith in the area of counselling.[21] They were encouraged in their writing by those who like to focus their ministry on the effects of the cults (and in particular by Dave Hunt, author of *The cult explosion* who writes in the foreword that 'I highly endorse the Bobgans' research and conclusion.' It appears that Christian writers can be substantially agreed on the issues surrounding the subject of hypnosis, start from a combination of biblical teaching and current evidence from science, and yet come to utterly different conclusions.

The Bobgans' critique has been followed more recently by *Slaying in the Spirit* by Nader Mikhaiel,[22] first privately published in 1992 and revised in 1995 to take account of the phenomena of the Toronto Blessing. Mikhaiel has carried out an amazing amount of amateur sleuthing to bring together information about the history and manifestations of hypnosis. These are then related to the phenomenon of recent movements such as the Toronto Blessing and the ministries of Rodney Howard-Browne and Kenneth Hagin. Mikhaiel writes from a solid understanding of the biblical text, and draws significantly on the literature of hypnosis. Yet he comes to a conclusion diametrically opposed to that of Dr Patrick Dixon, a British medical practitioner whose *Signs of revival* examines the Toronto Blessing phenomena from a scientific/biblical perspective.[23]

---

20 ibid. p. 53.

21 Bobgan, M. & D. (1972), *The psychological way/The spiritual way* (Minneapolis, MN: Bethany House).

22 Mikhaiel, N. (1995), *The Toronto Blessing: Slaying in the Spirit: The telling wonder* (Marrickville, NSW: Southville Press).

23 Dixon, P. (1994), *Signs of revival* (Eastbourne: Kingsway).

If such differences seem surprising, we need to see the issue in a broader context. Hypnosis is but one of a number of issues about which convinced Christians honestly differ, while looking at similar bodies of evidence. Current hot topics such as homosexuality, abortion and the ordination of women are three issues that have parallels to hypnosis. Divergence of final opinion arises after several stages of prior choices about what evidence is acceptable and how different kinds of evidence are to be weighed. With hypnosis, as with these other examples, we find several factors operating:

(a) Biblical sources are meagre and open to alternative translations of the actual text.

(b) Methods of interpretation of the biblical text vary greatly. A literal interpretation of the text brings different conclusions from those who contextualize it. Inferences about what a passage really means, and what we are to understand by the silences of Scripture also lead to divergences.

(c) Interpretation of key passages varies with literal fundamentalists differing from main-line evangelicals; with liberal interpreters differing from conservative interpreters; with Catholics differing from Protestants; and combinations of these groupings.

(d) The scientific evidence varies in quality and type. Some favour experiments, some rely on personal anecdotes; some accept data uncritically if it is 'scientific', whereas others challenge the methodology and assumptions that can result in bad science.

(e) Even if we were ever to agree that we have good biblical data, unambiguously interpreted, and good scientific data meticulously collected and reported, there would still be differences on how to weigh these very different sources to draw moral or ethical conclusions.

Why Christians disagree about hypnosis

This final chapter is intended to offer some direction to those who are confused by the many apparently contradictory messages about hypnosis from people who appear to know what they are talking about. To be told, on one hand, that hypnosis is an expression of normality, and can be therapeutic and spiritually enriching, while being told, on the other hand, that it is occultic, demonic and damaging at best, requires some clarification.

The position adopted here, and among the scientific community, is that hypnosis is one expression of altered states of consciousness (ASCs), and that these are normal manifestations, occurring with or without spiritual connotations. Such experiences are to be expected under certain conditions such as heightened expectation and suggestion. Dixon, in offering an understanding of charismatic phenomena, takes the position that ASCs are quite natural and it helps us to understand the spiritual manifestations if we understand the mechanisms by which they are expressed. He says: 'ASCs are generally regarded negatively in the western culture and little research has been carried out in this field. Yet I believe it is the key to making sense of Christian experience, particularly what is happening in many churches today.'[24] In marked contrast, Mikhaiel comes to the conclusion that 'contrary to scientific thinking, hypnosis does not seem to be an ordinary emotional behaviour. It does not seem to be natural. Hypnosis does not form an integral part of our normal life and does not conform to psychobiological laws.'[25] My commentary on such differences comes from a conviction that hypnosis can have value, while recognizing that something so powerful can also have attendant dangers. The following are some of the reasons why writers disagree over the evidence.

Stereotypical thinking is characteristically 'either/or'.

Objections to hypnosis commonly have a black-or-white quality to them. It is argued that if something is associated with false religions, it must therefore be evil. Something that can have a harmful influence on people must be bad. The Bobgans provide anecdotes linking hypnosis to religious practices and to negative outcomes in order to warn against the practice. Apparently lacking personal experience they refer to the warnings of Dennis and Rita Bennett in *The Holy Spirit and you* in the light of 'A case of a teenage girl whose behavior changed dramatically after an innocent exposure to hypnotism.'[26]

The apparent dangers expressed here need to be set in context since, if proven, they deserve serious consideration. It would be satisfying to read a carefully documented series of cases showing the links between hypnosis and harm. Failing that, a first-hand description of particular cases establishing the kind of harm and the circumstances under which hypnosis occurred would be far more convincing than a second-hand anecdote.

---

24 ibid. p. 260.
25 Mikhaiel, *The Toronto Blessing*, p. 60.
26 Bobgan, 'Hypnosis and the Christian', p. 52.

The Bobgans show at this point a singular lack of understanding of what constitutes evidence of harm. They report not many cases, but one. The case they select is not from their own experience but derived from the Bennetts' book which was published more than ten years before their own. We may ask: has nothing further come to light in a decade?! When we turn to the Bennetts' own description, there are more difficulties, since the case reported is not their own either. Nor do we actually know very much of relevance at all. In addition to the Bobgans' description, the Bennetts tell us:

> At a recent conference, a Christian leader who works with disturbed young people told of dealing with a teenage girl, the daughter of a Methodist minister, who had been hypnotized, at the age of eleven, at a Christmas program in her father's church. This was just a for fun thing – an amateur hypnotist at a party, and certainly no harm was intended. The girl, however, behaved abnormally from that point. Her whole personality changed; her parents were unable to reach her. She became involved in some serious misbehavior, including car theft. At the age of fourteen, she was ministered to for deliverance, and was set free from the spirit that had moved into her personality when she innocently submitted to hypnotism.[27]

From this single example, the Bennetts derived a sweeping conclusion 'Do not allow yourself to be hypnotized for any reason whatsoever.'[28]

Such an example provides no basis for drawing any conclusions about hypnosis, or a Christian understanding of what it involves. Yet, a whole theology of hypnosis is here constructed on an unpublished, unverified anecdote which is itself open to many alternative interpretations. It would be at least as rational to argue from this account regarding the dangers of Christmas parties, being born into a minister's household, or even of developing into adolescence! We should, in other words, ask the question whether this negative outcome was actually caused by hypnotic experience, or something else concurrent. Was the hypnosis used professionally and ethically by a skilled person? Clearly not in this example. Were these consequences psychological in nature or spiritual? Were these even consequences at all, or unrelated events? Anecdotes can provide food for thought, but are most unhelpful in trying to come to conclusions of a general kind. To the credit of the Bennetts, who claimed no special knowledge of hypnosis, they prefaced their book with the caution that 'We do not claim or believe that we have all the truth, nor are we sure that in the coming years

---

27 Bennett, *The Holy Spirit and you*, p. 50.
28 ibid. p. 50.
29 ibid. p. 8.

some of our views may not change, but we have presented these teachings sincerely and in the light we have at this time.'[29] Would that their opinions had not permeated so widely, twenty-five years after their writing, when so much more is known. A balanced appraisal will include asking whether hypnosis, when carefully used, produces more benefit than harm to an acceptable level. The current research on harmful effects of hypnosis supports that, in relation to physical and psychological outcomes, harmful effects occur very rarely. It is irresponsibly misleading to make sweeping generalizations from an example such as quoted above.[30]

By way of corrective balance I was able to engage in dialogue with Rita Bennett, who has continued an active healing ministry since the death of her husband. Asked about the above quotation, she attributed the absolutist stance to Dennis and indicated that she has had opportunity to give further thought to hypnosis. She followed our conversation with a letter, saying

> I think one of the main criticisms of hypnotism is yielding your will to another on a very deep level. It seems a prayer of protection over the will would be a valuable thing to do before therapy – especially for the Christian. In a number of instances when praying for people to be released in the Holy Spirit and to pray in the Spirit, as St Paul called it, Dennis and I found it was impossible for them to be freed in their prayer language until they renounced being hypnotized. This was not suggested to the person being prayed with, but was discovered through a process of elimination. Could we consider that there are those in Christ and those not in Christ practicing hypnotherapy? And could their spiritual influence touch their client deeply either for good or for ill depending on the therapist's orientation? If a Christian hypnotherapist worked with these people, it is probable that they would not have been blocked in the release of the Spirit. If the Christian hypno-therapist had also led these persons in a prayer of protection and yielding their will to God first, before therapy, they would have been doubly protected. Perhaps these ideas will offer some answers for the Christians in this field.[31]

Such thoughts could be reassuring and helpful to those who have previously seen hypnosis in totally negative terms.

Mikhaiel also engages in either/or thinking to pursue his argument, though his purpose is rather different. Whereas the Bobgans were setting out to show that hypnosis is dangerously anti-Christian, Mikhaiel's real

---

[29] ibid. p. 8.

[30] For an experiment to test the possibility of harm, and to explore other possible explanations, see Asha Singh, *Positive and negative effects in hypnosis: Some contributing variables*, Paper presented to the American Psychological Association Annual Convention, Los Angeles, August 1994.

[31] Personal communication, 1994.

target is the manifestations of the charismatic movement. He first seeks to equate phenomena of hypnosis with what is seen in the renewal movement, and makes many convincing parallels. By matching a list of hypnotic phenomena, borrowed from Dixon, who acknowledges Ludwig, he takes each hypnotic manifestation and shows how charismatic phenomena are comparable. His first conclusion is reductionist, seeking to argue that, with such a parallel, the charismatic expressions are nothing but hypnotically induced phenomena. He calls into question the spiritual nature of the Toronto Blessing by saying that instead of a profound experience of God, people are merely being hypnotized. This takes us to our next concern.

The spiritual dimension in hypnosis

The possibility that God can intervene in people's lives, and that this might be experienced through the normal phenomena of ASCs is embraced by Dixon but rejected by Mikhaiel because there is a second step to his argument. It is not sufficient to dismiss the spiritual as merely secular. He wants to show that hypnosis is demonic, and at this point he joins forces with the Bobgans. His dual rejection of hypnosis is expressed succinctly: 'Hypnosis not only is contrary to the order and will of the Creator, but is also intimately linked to the occult . . . There is clearly an occult power behind hypnosis with the variety of its physical, psychological and supernatural manifestations. It is apparent then that hypnosis is synonymous with what the Bible calls divination.' And so the trap is sprung! The Pentecostals are all in a state of hypnosis, and hypnosis is occultic, so we can discuss the Toronto Blessing and similar manifestations as a terrible departure from the truth. Readers of Mikhaiel's book would find that there is but a remnant of the church left untouched by his criticisms. He includes David Cho, Kenneth Hagin, John Wimber, John White, Francis McNutt, together with Wesley, Finney, Whitefield and Edwards, in his sights, and appears to speak favourably only of Dr Billy Graham.

The Bobgans address the same concerns in two ways in their chapter entitled 'Hypnosis: Medical, scientific or mystical?' to emphasize that we must not only ask scientific questions about hypnosis, but also look at possible spiritual dangers. Drawing on the writings of the missiologist Kurt Koch (see Chapter 5) they indicate that apparent clinical benefits are actually spiritually harmful. Koch believes that the power behind occult healing is demonic, that such healing serves as an impediment

---

[32] Bobgan, 'Hypnosis and the Christian', p. 47.

to a person's spiritual life, and that the damage is immense.[32] He derives this opinion from many years working among religious groups in South-East Asia who use hypnosis in their religious practices. They support this further with the opinion of Weldon and Levitt (whose credentials are unfortunately not identified), who are quoted by Mikhaiel as saying, 'Psychic healing . . . is a distinctly supernatural, spiritistic power and carries grave consequences, both for those who practice it and for those healed by it.'[33]

In drawing on these sources, it should be noted that the term 'hypnosis' does not appear. The guilt by association with the occult and psychic healing arises from the authors' prior linkage with these other practices to conclude that hypnosis is fatally enmeshed in these practices – the same guilt-by-association used by Mikhaiel. These objections then, are not against hypnosis at all! They are against the healing work of practitioners from other religious backgrounds. We should not be surprised if someone involved in witchcraft is impressed enough by a healing to be drawn more fully into that religious tradition. If New Age practitioners bring about valued changes in people, such people will surely be more likely to endorse the assumptions of New Age religion.

We all respond favourably to whatever brings the benefits we are looking for, but this is not enough to indicate whether we are dealing with something good or evil. The possibility that exposure to an influence such as hypnosis used by non-Christian practitioners will lead people away from the Christian faith is something I can readily endorse. But I would also want to say that the same techniques used by a Christian practitioner might have the effect of enhancing the faith of a Christian exposed to this influence. I would go further and say that my clinical experience over thirty years lends support to this view. The case histories presented in Chapters 4 and 6 are intended to be representative examples of that possibility.

The logic of this possibility is not lost on the Bobgans who proceed with their rhetorical questions to say: 'Let those Christians who call it scientific explain why they also recommend that it be performed by a Christian. If hypnosis is science indeed, why the added requirement of Christianity for the practitioner?'[34] This is a fair question, to which at least two things need to be said beyond what has already been incorporated in Chapter 4. Firstly, implied in the question there is once more a stereotypical separating out of science and religion as being

---

[33] ibid. p. 47.
[34] ibid. p. 48.

somehow distinct entities. Science is the pursuit of knowledge following certain rules of enquiry. Hypnosis is a particular technique for achieving an altered state of consciousness. It is possible to pursue scientific knowledge from a Christian perspective, or a secular one, or a Buddhist one, or a Marxist one, etc. It is possible to practise hypnosis from a secular standpoint, or as part of an occult practice, or within a Christian worldview. Hypnosis, of itself, is neither Christian nor secular.

Hence, the second point is that it is indeed wise for a Christian to seek out another Christian when help is required for problems that have moral and ethical implications. The practice of therapy, with or without hypnosis, is not value-free and a shared world view goes a long way in bringing help. So whether it is therapy or counselling, there are sound reasons for seeking a Christian practitioner. Rather than condemn hypnosis unequivocally, this line of reasoning surely indicates that such a powerful technique is best harnessed and used within a clearly formulated world view.

Valuing the opportunity to work with a Christian is not intended to devalue the competence or effectiveness of other practitioners to provide good quality care, since much training includes respect for the values of others even when they are very different from our own. Christian people often go to secular therapists and receive a great deal of benefit, without negative spiritual consequences. When it comes to the application of hypnotic techniques for procedural problems like pain management, I would prefer help from a well-trained ethical therapist with a secular world view to help from an under-trained Christian with poorly developed ethical standards. This is a personal opinion, not a prescription.

A more practical issue arises for the reader who is persuaded that hypnosis may be safe and who wants to seek help from someone trained in the use of it. Recognizing the dangers that can exist from practitioners who lack training or skills, with doubtful ethics or a world view that is not Christian, is it possible to find a reliable practitioner? The best answer to this difficulty is to find a trusted person who will provide a recommendation. Most medical practitioners, dentists, and psychologists know those who are practising hypnosis, and something of their reputation. Some pastors also have a network of contacts which include those who practise hypnosis. If these personal linkages are unsuccessful, then it is worth contacting one of the professional associations that maintain lists of practitioners. A brief list of the major ones is included in Appendix 2.

World view as an issue

The arguments marshalled against hypnosis make a good deal more sense when they are focused to become an argument for a soundly based world view. The objections to becoming involved in the occult are valid because they stand over against the Christian world view. How a person gets involved in the occult is less important than the outcome.

To make the distinction clearer, we may ask how people become involved in Scientology. A primary contact for seeking adherents has been to offer completion of a personality test to passers-by and use the results to indicate that only through Scientology will their identified personal problems be resolved. When it comes to technique, there is a close parallel between 'Fill out this form and come to Scientology to save you', and the practice of handing out gospel tracts and saying, 'Come to Jesus and he will save you.' What really matters is not the technique, but what lies behind it, provided the technique itself is ethical. Whether through hypnosis, or other therapeutic techniques, or through counseling, change can occur. World view is a critical component in determining the relative benefits of the changes brought about when spiritual values are at stake.[35]

This is exactly Mikhaiel's point. His urgent warning is that the charismatic phenomena do not represent an encounter with the Holy Spirit but with the devil. According to Mikhaiel's own criteria, Billy Graham remains untarnished because 'there appears to be no evidence that those attending his crusades demonstrate such phenomena as falling to the ground, jerking, spontaneous laughing, experiencing catalepsy or any of the other hypnotic spontaneous manifestations that simply present themselves without any suggestion. Yet we do not find one case of typical hypnosis despite such conducive environment for hypnosis, where there is a lot of singing, prayer and music.'[36] Alternatively, we may say that the preaching of Billy Graham occurred at a time between revivals – after Azusa and before Toronto – and his ministry represents an ongoing faithfulness in a period when the Holy Spirit was not being manifested in the same manner. His preaching also had expectations – for personal commitment to faith, expressed initially by moving to the front for counselling. It is the testimony of many who responded that they felt an inner conviction and compulsion to respond in this way.

---

[35] This emphasis on a soundly-based world view is developed by G. Collins (1993), *The biblical basis of Christian counseling for people helpers* (Colorado Springs, CO: NavPress).
[36] Mikhaiel, *The Toronto Blessing*, p. 60.

George Matheson, a Canadian professor of psychology, has argued that such crusades have all the ingredients for hypnotic induction, and clearly differs from Mikhaiel in his interpretation of the response of those who attend: 'Simultaneous sensory experiences including a bright glow, an inner voice, or a spiritual force nudging and guiding are all phenomena consistent with the activity of a dissociated processing state [trance]. This effect may be terminated by the dramatic change in the environment at the close of the service, or it may linger as evidenced in the faces and behaviour of some leaving the crusades.'[37]

The therapeutic dimension of hypnosis

Some like to dismiss the problem of hypnosis by saying that hypnosis really does not exist, or, if it does, it cannot be reliably distinguished from other altered states. If there is no such thing as hypnosis, then these vigorous defences deserve no further discussion. Difficulties of definition certainly exist, but this does not mean hypnosis is non-existent. That it is one among a range of ASCs makes precise differentiation a problem, but scientific advances are clearing up some of that ambiguity.

Assuming it does exist, the Bobgans downplay its significance by quoting Kaplan and Friedman's *Textbook of psychiatry*, 'Everything done in psychotherapy with hypnosis can also be done without hypnosis.'[38] That appears to be true. Certainly many clinicians believe it. So should we abandon it? What is not said here is that while the outcome can be the same, the use of hypnosis can bring results more quickly, less painfully and much less expensively. When people also learn to be empowered to continue using what they have learned, the risk of relapse is reduced. It is now little more than an indulgent luxury of a wealthy minority to receive therapy for months or years at a time (allowing exceptions for some serious conditions that cannot be helped quickly). The current emphasis in health care is on achieving good outcomes in the shortest possible time. Hypnosis can play a significant part in achieving this.

There is a large body of clinical evidence that hypnosis can produce excellent results. At that point, however, I come up against the Bobgans quite different opinion: 'Results should not be evidence for promoting and utilising hypnotism. Immediate positive results from hypnotism should especially be dismissed as evidence for validity of the practice, since

---

37 Matheson, 'Hypnotic aspects of religious experiences.

38 Bobgan, 'Hypnosis and the Christian', p. 47.

many who gain initial victory over problems later suffer defeat.'[39] So are we to reject successful therapy because some people relapse? The medical profession, with a commitment to life, suffers a 100 per cent failure rate! Relapse prevention is a recognized area of clinical study, identifying how relapse can be reduced. But no one wants to advocate only those therapies that always work for everyone. Unfortunately, the allegation that relapse might be a problem is supported by quoting a study on headaches, in which two-thirds reported symptom substitution. The example would have been more convincing if hypnosis had been the treatment method. In actuality, the patients had been treated with biofeedback![40] Certainly, relapse does occur in all therapies but we continue for the sake of those who benefit. If we take a walk along to the local church and ask about the effectiveness of evangelism, we find there too that many are changed for good yet in that context we find some fall away. Do we stop preaching or do we find means to minimize the problem?

At one point in this discussion I can agree with the Bobgans when they challenge the pragmatism of those who say, 'Since it works it must be good.' I share their rejection of such an argument and prefer to reverse it to say, 'If it's good, it must work.' If we take this same aphorism across to Mikhaiel's contentions about the charismatic phenomena there is a serious problem for the church. He is addressing them from the position that they do indeed work – that slaying in the Spirit, speaking in tongues, etc. are genuinely occurring in the context of the Toronto Blessing. Unfortunately, by labelling these phenomena 'occultic', one has to draw the conclusion that it works, and it is bad. Ultimately, Mikhaiel's allegation is one of wholesale apostasy. The major area of growth of the Christian church throughout the world is found in the Pentecostal and charismatic traditions: this is the most vibrant and energetic expression of Christendom today. To suggest that the whole movement is ultimately corrupted by divination and demonic powers is a sweeping indictment. An alternative view is that there is a flaw in his argument, and hundreds of millions are actually rejoicing in the work of the Holy Spirit expressed in new ways.

To choose or not to choose

The issue of choice and free will is of such importance that I have returned to it several times. It deserves a brief return here, since it is also taken

[39] ibid. p. 46.
[40] This is not my inference but is mentioned in the text: see ibid. p. 46.

seriously by the Bobgans. With their customary rhetorical questions, they head Chapter 4 with 'Can the will be violated in hypnosis?' and their first chapter with 'Hypnosis: How much deception?'

To their first question, the answer is clearly yes. And that answer is as useful as answering yes to the question, 'Can an overdose of drugs kill you?' The stereotype of manipulative hypnosis is raised to imply some Machiavellian monster taking over the will and forcing people against their will to do that which is contrary to their own moral values. Could that happen? Yes. And could we ever envisage the pastor of a church so controlling the people that they would act against their own moral values at his behest? The Jonestown episode tells me: Yes. The better question is: '*Does* it happen?' I have argued above that ethically practised hypnosis enhances freedom of choice, and empowers the person being hypnotized. The stereotype born out of Mesmer's day should not cause us to abandon that which can be valuable.

The Bobgans also raise two more levels of discussion which deserve attention, namely the area of rationality and unconscious processes, and the concern about suggestion and deception.

RATIONALITY AND UNCONSCIOUS PROCESSES

The Bobgans raise the concern that when a person moves from rational logical thought across to the more creative and spontaneously vivid world of right hemisphere functioning there is a dangerous loss of control over the will. They write: 'Because hypnosis places responsibility outside the exercise of objective, rational, fully conscious choice it does violate the will. The normal evaluating abilities are submerged and choice is made according to suggestion without the balance of rational restraint.'[41]

This a commonly held stereotype reflects some peculiar assumptions of Western intellectualism. The primacy of reason and controlled logic is greatly prized within the scientific traditions of Western thought, but is in no sense a universal statement about the best in human thinking. This is a strongly male view of reality, and rewarded in Western educational systems. At the same time there is the remarkably pervasive influence of the Freudian tradition which has stressed both the strength of the unconscious and its dangers as the repository of the uncontrolled urges of the id. Or, in more Christian terms, the lusts and passions of the sinful nature are seen to lurk there waiting to escape and overwhelm the higher functions of ego and super-ego.

---

41 ibid. p. 35.

Perhaps here we see that the Bobgans, who for so long have argued vehemently against Freudian psychology and against the primacy of science over biblical thinking, are themselves absorbing these very principles. To be arguing against the use of hypnosis because of its capacity to unleash the dreaded unconscious is a tasteful irony if we acknowledge that it was the powerful benefits of hypnosis (which Freud saw demonstrated by Bernheim in Paris) that provided him with one of his most compelling reasons for believing in the unconscious.[42]

Mikhaiel is also concerned about violation of the will by the use of hypnosis, and casts this in the same Freudian mode of a battle between the conscious and the unconscious. He cites examples of powerful effective suggestions, such as Rasputin's famous after-dinner trick of hypnotizing the palace guard and leaving them propped up around the courtyard. The example would be more convincing if it could be shown that the wills of these soldiers had been violated. One might ask whether they willingly entered into the atmosphere of participating, as occurs in stage hypnosis. Instead Mikhaiel asks, more ominously, 'Is this natural? More importantly is this the intention of the Creator?'[43]

A short response is that this response is entirely natural. It conforms to laws of nature as we are gradually coming to understand them, and there is no need to invoke any supernatural explanation at all. It is not clear whether the Creator wills for soldiers to be out of action in the evening. Behind the question lies a concern about the Creator's use of hypnosis in any setting. On this point, Mikhaiel disagrees with the Bobgans who do consider that hypnosis was used by the Creator when it is recorded in Genesis 2:21 that 'The Lord God caused a deep sleep to fall upon the man, and while he slept took one of his ribs.' This presents a problem for Mikhaiel who remarks that God never uses trances for the purpose of healing, and he has to explain this passage away by saying that putting Adam into a deep sleep simply means Adam was neither an observer nor a partaker of the act of creation. This fails to do justice to the Hebrew text which is quite explicit. The term *tardemah* is used here and refers to 'deep sleep'. It is cognate with the modern Hebrew usage of *heerdeem*, to put to sleep, or anaesthetize, and *hardamah*, meaning anaesthesia. Although there were undoubtably other ways the Creator could have undertaken the creation of Eve it is reassuring to suppose that the hypnotic state was used for such an auspicious occasion.

---

42 See Scroggs, J. R. (1985), *Key ideas in personality theory* (St Paul, MN: West Publishing), p. 14.

43 Mikhaiel, *The Toronto Blessing*, p. 64.

It is quite unnecessary to postulate that in hypnosis the unconscious has taken over and the powers of volitional control have been sacrificed. The more recent evidence from brain research leads us to understand it as a shift in the focus of activity in the brain (see Chapter 1), generating a different but not lesser kind of thinking. Such thought processes can be enriching and powerful, in contrast to the model of hypnosis accessing evil depths of unconscious desires. Rather than opening the gate to evil, there can be a further experience of healthy spirituality (see Chapter 5).[44]

Ernest Rossi proposed some years ago that 'If the metaphor of conscious and unconscious could be translated to the metaphor of dominant and non-dominant hemispheres, there may be a neurological basis for describing a new hypnotherapeutic approach.'[45] This newer understanding can be appreciated through an excerpt from Wanda Poltawska, a physician who writes from the Institute for the Theology of the Family in Krakow, Poland:

> Many authors, with Freud, regard the unconscious as an anonymous distinctive power to which we yield and which in a subtle but essential manner determines our behavior. Doctors often speak about this power, and patients often try to justify their conduct by appealing to it: psychiatrists and psychotherapists share this opinion. It is often difficult to free the patient from the oppressive feeling of this determination. Karol Wojtyla [Pope John Paul II] on the other hand understands the unconscious as part of the potentiality of the human person; part of the task which each of us resolves personally, making it conscious and subject to the person's self-determination. According to Karol Wojtyla the role of the unconscious is: a) Making visible our potentiality and the perspective of our development. b) Showing us our inner constitution and coherence of the subject. By enclosing and conserving everything we experience, it enriches us and furnishes material for conscious elaboration. It shows us as creatures innately subjected to time, and as the unconscious strives towards consciousness, it serves our integration. This stage which is at variance with the psychoanalytical doctrine, has been confirmed in practice and by the so-called experiment of life.[46]

---

[44] For a contemporary psychological exploration of this theme, see Epstein, S. (1994), 'Integration of the cognitive and the psychodynamic unconscious', *American Psychologist, 49*, 8, 709–24.

[45] Erickson, M. H. & Rossi, E. L. (eds) (1980), *The collected papers of Milton H. Erickson on hypnosis: Vol I. The nature of hypnosis and suggestion* (New York: Irvington), quoted in Mathews, W. J., Lankton, S. & Lankton, C., 'An Ericksonian model of hypnotherapy', Chapter 9, in Rhue, Lynn & Kirsch, *Handbook of clinical hypnosis*.

[46] Poltawska, W. (1992), 'Objectifying Psychotherapy', *Catholic Medical Quarterly, 42*, 4, 18–23.

In these terms, hypnosis can serve as a vehicle for gaining easier access to those creative and integrational aspects of human experience which often elude our conscious life, yet are all-too-briefly sensed in our moments of great joy, as well as in our dreams. We can see that, from this position, erosion of the will is not an issue. If anything, the reverse is true.

SUGGESTION AND DECEPTION

The erosion of conscious choice by being placed under the will of the hypnotist is also proposed by the Bobgans as a further danger. In a step-like progression in their chapter 'Hypnosis: How much deception?' they move through three phases of answering their own question. Firstly raising the spectre that 'deception may enter in', they proceed to the rhetorical 'Is this merely suggesting or is it deception?' to conclude their chapter with 'Hypnosis . . . relies heavily on . . . both direct and indirect deception.'[47]

Whereas suggestion is a central term, and frequently identified as a central element of hypnosis, deception is a negatively laden term with innuendos of deliberately misleading people for evil intentions. The idea that people are deceived in hypnosis sits well with the view that they are helplessly passive and under external control. Indeed, there are dangers to be avoided, but this can mean that we either avoid hypnosis altogether, or we use it with wise discernment. This requires the use of the critical faculties.

In this connection I am indebted to a former student, Nancy Rivas, for the following comments concerning laying aside the critical faculties:

> I think that the Bible encourages and even requires this in some ways (e.g. waiting on the Lord), but it also encourages and requires some safety nets to be in place. For instance, the testing of the spirits in John, the moral guidelines of Scripture, the feedback of the community, the confirmation of many different sources and experiences pointing in the same direction – all these things are also a strong part of Christian life, and are in part what makes it safe to open oneself up to the more subjective spiritual experiences, because there are checks and balances in the biblical model to keep one from becoming self-destructive or hurtful to others or heretical.

It is the job of Christian therapists who wish to utilize hypnosis to try to put functionally similar safety nets in place to protect the emotional and spiritual wellbeing of their clients who make themselves so vulnerable – and to follow the biblical guidelines for safety for themselves as well. It also follows that to allow oneself to be hypnotized by a therapist who

---

47 Bobgan,'Hypnosis and the Christian', p. 20.

does not set up and submit to such safety guidelines may be emotionally and spiritually dangerous.

Both hypnotic methods and spiritual experiences produce powerful and speedy healing, with or without insight. In part, their impact derives from a common mechanism. Both utilize the active – receptive – noncritical state, which by-passes defences and disbelief and allows the therapeutic words (of the therapist or God) to impact the deep levels of the person relatively directly.

The stereotype of mind manipulation is misleading. Certainly, changed perceptions and beliefs can occur in response to hypnotic suggestion. That is exactly why the therapist turns to hypnosis. But believing something differently is not the same as being deceived. Indeed, Christians and others readily acknowledge that the source of many of their difficulties can be found in their distorted belief systems.[48] Seeing reality in a new way is often healthier psychologically and spiritually than seeing it through the old blinkers of sin or sickness.[49]

Sometimes acceptable?

Briefly adapting the questioning style of the Bobgans (which invades their every chapter and casts more doubt than light on the subject) it is worth repeating that, for all their steadfast refusal to see anything but evil in hypnosis, they do acknowledge that there are Christian writers willing to embrace the value of hypnosis practised by those who are qualified. They cite Walter Martin of the Christian Research Institute, with a special interest in cult activity, as saying that he endorses the use of hypnosis by medical doctors; they also cite McDowell and Stewart (authors of *Understanding the occult)* as saying the same.[50] The missionary Kurt Koch is quoted as distinguishing medical uses of hypnosis from their occultic applications, but their claim that Koch rejects medical hypnosis is at odds with Koch's own position: 'Our concern at the moment is not with the professional use of hypnosis . . . [but as]. . . used by magic charmers and unqualified medical practitioners.'[51]

---

[48] The importance of changed thinking as a key element in successful counselling is developed in Wright, H. N. (1986), *Self-talk, imagery and prayer in counseling*. (Dallas, TX: Word).

[49] For a very thorough examination of the subjective experience of being in hypnotic trance, see Sheehan & McConkey, *Hypnosis and experience*.

[50] Bobgan, 'Hypnosis and the Christian', p. 14.

[51] Koch as quoted in ibid. p. 47. (Koch's words, 'I reject even the kind of hypnosis used by doctors', make his own position unclear).

Of course there are many more professionals who are Christians who will use and advocate the use of hypnosis. Indeed, it is an unusual fringe minority who will continue, even today, to advance the stereoptypical objections from the past as if they represent eternal truth. However, there is one last and important reason why this hostile stance continues to be maintained.

Back to the Bible

This chapter started by referring to the sources which might be drawn on to determine our position on hypnosis, noting that disagreements can occur for various intertwining reasons. Most of the debate on this subject is ostensibly concerned with evidences from science, yet at the very heart of it all, the real issue for Christians is a biblical and spiritual one. The dangers that hypnosis might be used to manipulate, and that the therapeutic claims may be false, are trivial addenda if we assert that, first and foremost, the use of hypnosis is condemned in Scripture. If hypnosis is in essence one of a range of occultic practices, all of which always lead the participants away from faith in God, then the cautions of the Bobgans are well-founded and deserve serious attention.

A more balanced view comes from Roger Mesmer, a Christian physician who recognizes the dangers of hypnosis and who comments that the Scriptures distinguish between altered states that enhance a person's access to God and those that constitute occult practices. Prophets and apostles entered trances and visionary states (Num. 24:4; Dan. 2:19; Acts 10:10; 11:15; 22:17; Rev. 1:10) . . . Some other altered state procedures, such as mediumship, are expressly forbidden. Deuteronomy 18:10–11 also proscribes being or dealing with enchanters, witches and wizards.[52] How disappointing it is to find that the only biblical foundation that is ever offered for condemning hypnosis is Deuteronomy 18:11. Having identified hypnosis (or, to use their preferred but antiquated term, hypnotism) with all things occult, the Bobgans use this as the basis for attacking a range of activities, even including sideswipes against biofeedback and acupuncture, though thankfully finding no verse of Scripture against them!

We should not lose sight of the dangers of occultic healing practices even though hypnosis does not have to be one of them. The key question revolves not around a misinterpreted phrase in the Old Testament, but

---

[52] Mesmer, R. (1987). 'Hypnosis induced by a hypnotist', *Journal of Christian Healing*, 9, 1, 51–3.

around the more significant general issue to which the Bobgans address themselves. They capture the essence of the biblical objections to charmers and others when they say, 'All forms of the occult turn a person away from God to self and to those spirits who are in opposition to God.'[53] That is indeed well said. We may then test the validity of the case of hypnosis by seeing what happens when we move from the general to the particular. Is it correct to state that all forms of hypnosis turn a person away from God to self and to those spirits who are in opposition to God? To that, many witnesses will offer a resounding 'No!'

If we take that same question across to those involved with the Toronto Blessing, which is said to be an example of hypnosis in action, then it should follow that all who have been involved there are subject to occult forces and have been turned away from God. If one test of spirits is that of fruitfulness, then there is no basis for saying that all hypnotic experiences are occultic. A renewed passion for relationship with God is the more common response of those involved in renewal.

On a more positive note

A PARALLEL

I have read and heard many criticisms of the Christian faith from unbelievers. I am embarrassed at times at the behaviour of some who claim to act in the name of Christ, from the collective behaviour of the Inquisition to the sexual molestation of little children by clergy. Yet I continue to believe the gospel, and see such behaviour as coming from distortions of the truth, not an expression of it. I see Christians believing in peace, yet and engaging in war. I see church leaders manipulating their followers to give money, only to use it to personal advantage. I see Christian marriages shattered, even though I read that God hates divorce. I see people who believe in the resurrection and the joy of new life behaving as if there were no hope, here or hereafter. And I believe in miracles, even when my scientific training suggests I am just being deceived.

If a scientist from another planet came to earth to conduct research on this strange group who call themselves Christians, they would have a hard time making any sense of it all. With so many discrepancies between beliefs and behaviour, could it be that the belief system is all wrong? I would want to suggest to the alien scientist that behind these sad

---

[53] ibid. p. 51

inconsistencies lies something that has stood the test of time – something rooted not in human fallibility but in God's omnipotence. Individual and collective failures abound, yet God is working out his purposes. I would want that scientist to see the big picture and avoid being sidetracked into focusing on the exceptions. I would warn of a danger that started in the Garden of Eden when the serpent insinuated doubts about God's goodness with 'Has God said...?' (Gen. 3). Asking rhetorical questions is a destructive exercise if no positive affirmations follow

THE BIGGER PICTURE

If you followed me in the preceding paragraph you may recognize why hypnosis has been the subject of attack by some, while others advocate its value. In a sinful world, God's gifts can be distorted. Our capacity to move from one level or one kind of consciousness to another is a rich gift allowing us a wonderful diversity of experiences. The artist becomes more creative; the athlete functions at peak performance; the worshipper enters into a foretaste of heaven; and those who suffer deep hurt find ways of surviving. All these experiences occur quite naturally and should not be attributed to hypnosis itself. There are similarities, but we must avoid the conclusion that because things are similar they are therefore the same. Hypnosis comes into the picture when those naturally occurring shifts are harnessed and facilitated, using the techniques mentioned in earlier chapters, to bring heightened awareness and enriched experience.

Let us acknowledge in passing that when we embrace something as natural this may be good, but the Bobgans do us a service in noting that our fallen nature means there can be things that are natural and not good. In this context I am claiming altered states to be part of our humanness, like changes in blood pressure, which exist as a part of our created nature, rather than evidence of our fallen nature.[54]

Suggestibility has been mentioned many times as a key component in making good use of the trance state. That word has several meanings, so we need to repeat that it refers not to gullibility (as might be supposed from the Bobgans' emphasis on deception), but rather the capacity to enter into imagining beyond what is to what might be. 'Envisioning possibilities' gets close to the meaning of the term, and that seems to come very close to a recurring theme of the Christian life. For example, 'It does not yet appear what we shall be like, but we know that when we see Him, we shall be like Him.' (1 Jn. 3:2).

---

[54] See ibid. Ch. 5 for their discussion of this topic.

Trust is a key component in the relationship developed in hypnosis. The unusually close relationship can develop into the kind of transference that scared Freud and decided him against hypnosis. For those who continue to insist that clinical objectivity and emotional distance is the way to help people, hypnosis is best avoided. However, there are many Christians who would believe that, at this point, as at many others, Freud got it wrong. My friend and colleague, Dr H. Newton Malony, professor at Fuller Seminary, expressed this well some years ago:

> Freud decried the transference/countertransference type relationship that hypnosis involved. He felt it compromised the neutrality of the therapist. According to Freud, the best therapy occurred when the therapist was a passive catalyst for the working out of the repressed feelings of the client. Hypnosis, at its best, involves a close relationship between hypnotist and client. As indicated earlier, research since the time of Freud has clearly indicated the importance of trust, empathy and warmth in preparing a person for trance inducement . . . The Hebrew meaning of knowledge is relationship. To know God is to have a personal encounter with him. If God is to be revealed through Christian persons, as I assume every religious hypnotist would affirm, then He is to be revealed through the relationship between therapist and client . . . Of course, there are dangers here, but the important thing to remember is that closeness and dependency and identification are not bad in and of themselves. In fact, for the Christian hypnotist they are integral to Christian witness.[55]

Another key component of hypnosis is said to be passivity. This feature bothers the Bobgans since it opens the possibility of control, loss of will, and manipulation of helplessness. I have been taught by my clients that there is actually a paradox here. While the hypnotic trance can be characterized by passivity, this does not preclude an active involvement in all that happens. Freedom of choice is not violated. The way this apparent passivity works may be understood better by thinking of receptivity – or willingness to listen, learn, absorb and use new insight. The trusting relationship of hypnosis allows a dialogue which enables a person to rethink and change. Since most of us are very poor listeners, there is much to be said for a state in which receptive listening is important. When Jesus said, 'He that has ears to hear, let him hear', he was recognizing that we often fail to listen effectively.

In this paradoxically active–passive state, heightened receptivity is paired with heightened alertness allowing for intensified critical thought and resulting in strategic responses. Those who follow the methods of Milton Erickson know that paradox is a powerful vehicle for induction

---

[55] Malony, H. N. (1983), 'A theology for hypnosis: A beginning enquiry', *Journal of Psychology and Christianity, 2*, 1, 2–11.

and production of therapeutic change. Those who follow the teachings of Jesus also know the power of paradox, as we wrestle with what it means that the one who loses life shall find it, and that the first shall be last.

Finally, there is in most hypnotic experiences a great deal of influence achieved through the use of carefully chosen words. Because the trance state is associated with primary process thinking (see Chapter 1) and with trance-logic, words are often interpreted very literally and have a power to change not often experienced at other times. Changes in emotional states can be achieved by the careful use of words. Phrases can be learned and repeated in hypnosis which provide support at later times when help is needed.

As Christians we have little need to be reminded of the power of words, nor the ultimate authority of the Word made flesh. In hypnosis it is possible to use words powerfully and to spend time in relationship with the Word. As the occult turns a person from God, so positive Christian intervention will turn people to God. I have described a few examples of this in earlier chapters. I finish with one example of a person whom I have seen move from darkness to light with the help of hypnosis.

Among many significant spiritual encounters, one case had to do specifically with words. This lady was a person of faith, a regular worshipper, who had suffered many serious abuses over the years. One day she asked to use hypnosis so that she could access some material from her teenage years. She had some conscious awareness of what she needed to deal with, but had recognized that hypnosis gave her permission to go to painful material safely. In trance she revealed an experience she had never dared mention in the intervening twenty-five years. Left alone by her parents, she was befriended by a neighbour who introduced her to some religious rituals which included reciting a secret mantra which should on no account be spoken to anyone else. Although she had left the influence of the person after quite a short time, she continued to be bound by the belief that she would come to harm if she ever spoke those words which continued to circle repetitively in her head. I assured her that in Christ she was now under a higher power, and that Jesus is God's Word to us. I instructed her to repeat the mantra aloud, which she did, after which I prayed with her for release from this oppression. There was immediate and obvious release, and she was able to speak about this. Spiritual and emotional growth began to occur and continued consistently.

Conclusions

Looking back over thirty years of work as a clinician, I am persuaded that hypnosis is a powerful tool in bringing about psychological change. The clinical literature is quite clear in providing evidence to document its effectiveness in treating conditions. A wider literature documents the ways in which healthy functioning people can be helped to become even more effective. Scientific research is gradually helping us to understand why this should be so, but there is a great deal still to be learned.

And there we might leave it if the topic were simply hypnosis and healing. By adding to the title 'and the Christian', other issues are immediately raised. It is important then to go beyond scientific research to recognize there are moral and ethical dimensions of behaviour which science rarely addresses. There are spiritual and religious issues which cause us not only to ask what is happening and how, but also why. The inherent dangers of a powerful technique that affects thinking, feeling, and behaviour cannot be discounted since anything powerful is open to abuse.

The possibility of being open to demonic influence in this setting cannot be dismissed as fanciful if we believe in the presence of evil. Under circumstances where people choose to relinquish their freedom of choice to those who use hypnotic techniques to exploit them, the risks are significant. We have also noted that such risks are not confined to the hypnotic states. There are many other altered states of consciousness, some of them fostered in Christian worship, where the potential for harm exists. Manipulation can occur even in the church, and even with the best of intentions.

Having acknowledged the risks, it is then essential to enquire about the evidence for such dangers, and at this point there is a pleasant surprise. Apart from observations among other religions, even those Christians writers who are most vehemently opposed to hypnosis fail to document examples that demonstrate their point. Occasional anecdotes provide food for thought but by their very scarcity and uncertainty, serve rather to emphasize how very safe hypnosis can be when used in an ethical and professional way. Indeed, evidences of people being led into confusion and false teaching by preachers are much more readily available.

Perhaps more extraordinary is the fact that strong condemnation of hypnosis can be brought forward by Christian writers with such a limited appeal to Scripture. If hypnosis is so hazardous, we should expect more than a passing reference to it in Scripture. Important principles are invariably given repeated attention. In the present situation, one isolated verse is brought forward, a verse that suffers from poor exegesis. Put simply, the Bible is silent on the dangers of hypnosis.

The word 'hypnosis' is modern. If we follow the Biblical material that appears to refer to hypnosis, words such as sleep and trance, we find a favourable linkage with its use by God as Creator, as well as the highly significant spiritual experiences of Peter and Paul. We may then be thankful for a technique which can prove so powerful in so many situations. Of itself, it is neither good nor bad. Many have found relief from problems through its use. Many have been able to draw nearer to God, to experience a deeper awareness of spirituality and to enrich their understanding of God's mercy. It is a tragedy that so many Christian people have been warned off hypnosis, when it has such great potential to provide benefit to body, mind, and spirit.

Appendix 1:

Hypnosis and Repressed Memories

There has been a great deal of confusion among therapists, and pain for many clients and their families, in the face of a recent escalation of reported repressed memories. These memories are associated with diagnoses of trauma, especially child sexual abuse (sometimes including stories of satanic ritual abuse), and appear frequently in those diagnosed as suffering from multiple personality disorder, (MPD), now renamed dissociative identity disorder, DID).

Hypnosis is relevant to this ongoing debate in that: (a) many believe that the mechanism of dissociation said to underlie these diagnoses is also the mechanism by which people in hypnosis achieve amnesia; (b) those with DID are said to be in a state of natural hypnosis, moving spontaneously between altered states as a coping mechanism; (c) many reported memories have been elicited only when the person is in a hypnotic trance state; (d) this large increase in the retrieving of repressed memories coincides with the increased therapeutic use of hypnosis, and with the more frequent diagnosis of MPD or DID.

While it may be argued that these related facts point to improved access to previously hidden but painful memories, allowing them to be brought forward and resolved, there is also the possibility that the process is actually creating or at least embellishing memories. A few therapists have been seeing many clients who report sustained trauma, accessing material of which they were previously unaware. Since many other therapists have not experienced the same increase, it is possible that subtle cues create expectations that have led to such reporting. Conversely, those who are finding these reports may argue that they are tapping into a previously hidden reality, which their colleagues are failing to detect.

A question at the heart of this ambiguity is whether the memories retrieved represent historical fact, or whether they represent something else. In this debate some distinguish 'historical truth' from 'narrative truth' to indicate that there could be clinical relevance to the memories even when they are not objectively verifiable.

As evidence has been coming forward, more has become known about how memory works, though a great deal is still uncertain. Experimental work, and studies using hypnosis, show that memory is fallible (people make mistakes), and it is malleable (events can be rewritten when recalled). Memory of emotionally significant material is very prone to change. Memory of events from many years ago is much more unreliable than recent recall.

A large added set of complications arises when people receiving therapy or inner healing are encouraged to go back by age-regression methods to find the early source of their problems. Not only do people in this situation want to find something themselves, but so also does the healer. This combined pressure from expectations and suggestions is especially powerful in an altered state, which is present whether formal hypnosis is being used, or the techniques of inner healing are being applied.

A further complicating factor has been the escalation effect arising from publicity given to dramatic accounts of abuse, presented as films and in books. As many people have been exposed to such films and books as *Sybil* or *When Rabbit howls*, as well as media accounts of people's reported experiences, it is possible for them to assimilate such materials so that they become the basis of supposed personal experiences. In other words, it is not necessary for a therapist even to implant ideas or ask leading questions when there is already a reservoir of poorly digested experience which is indistinguishable from personal memory. Research on altered states makes it clear that once such material has been accepted, it becomes difficult or impossible to discern the difference between actual events, confabulated recall, and the newly introduced experiences.

Hypnosis has been implicated in a significant number of cases where false memories have been alleged. A leading US hypnotherapist, Dr Peter Bloom, says that, when using hypnosis, 'false memories may result from premature assumptions, inept questioning, and loss of objectivity in the face of intense abreactions'. As a result there are dangers for those seeking for answers to their problems that, instead of achieving relief from past abuse, they will become fixed in a cycle of discovering more and more bizarre material. If what they find then serves as the basis for accusations against friends and family, the problem becomes greatly compounded for all concerned.

The 'False Memory Syndrome' is now being given serious attention by many groups in the community, and professional societies are taking these issues seriously. Organizations have developed, including the False Memory Syndrome Foundation in the USA, and the British False Memory Society, the latter being established in 1993. A good account of the concerns of families accused by patients was presented to members of the British Society of Clinical and Experimental Hypnosis by Roger Scotford, Director of the British group. Under a heading 'The myths', he referred to the following misconceptions:

1. That memories retrieved under hypnosis are more accurate than other memories.
2. That you can hypnotically or age regress someone back to their childhood without them taking their adult experience and fantasies with them.
3. That you can hypnotically regress someone back to an actual former life. (One BFMS member has been accused of abusing a niece in a former life.)
4. That it is a 'well known fact' that sustained episodes of childhood sexual abuse can be repressed and stored away in some inaccessible filing cabinet for decades, only then to be released by some therapeutic practice. It is not a fact, it is only an unproven theory. Forgetting is a fact: repression is a concept.
5. That memories can be stored in other parts of the body outside the brain. There is no neuro-biological evidence to show that this is possible.
6. That you can retrospectively 'diagnose' childhood sexual abuse in an adult from the psychological symptoms they currently present.
7. That perpetrators of abuse always deny the abuse when confronted with it.
8. That not only the victim repressed the memory of the abuse, but so did the perpetrator. Neither of them knew that the abuse occurred until the therapist 'uncovered' it.[1]

The difficulties in interpreting reports of early memories have led to several professional organizations setting up working groups to analyse the present state of knowledge, and provide guidelines for those who seek to understand what is happening. There is a good deal of overlap between the reports of these groups, while addressing the needs of diverse practitioners.

In particular, the serious reader is referred to:

1. The American Psychological Association Working Group.[2]

---

[1] Scotford, R. (1995). 'Myths, memories and reality', *Contemporary Hypnosis*, *12*, 2, 137–42.

[2] Preliminary reports were published in 1995. The final report appeared in *Psychological Hypnosis* (1996), and the final conclusions published by the American Psychological Association, and in the *Australian Journal of Clinical and Experimental Hypnosis* (May 1997), *25*, 1, 8–17.

2. The American Medical Association.[3]
3. The British Psychological Society.[4]
4. The Australian Psychological Society.[5]
5. Professor Kevin McConkey, President of the Australian Psychological Society for 1994, who is widely known for his experimental work on hypnosis. He devoted his presidential address to 'Hypnosis, memory and the ethics of uncertainty'.[6]

---

[3] American Medical Association (1995), 'Report on memories of childhood abuse'. *Contemporary Hypnosis 43*, 2, 114–17.

[4] Andrews, B., Morton, J., Bekerian, D. A., Brewin, C. R., Davies, G. M. & Mollon, P. (1995), 'The recovery of memories in clinical practice: Experiences and beliefs of British Psychological Society practitioners', *The Psychologist, 8*, 5, 209–14. 'Further comment on recovered memories', *The Psychologist, 8*, 11, 507–8. Toon, K., Fraise, J., McFetridge, M. & Alwin, N. (1996), 'Memory or mirage?: The FMS debate', *The Psychologist, 9*, 2, 73–7.

[5] The Australian Psychological Society (February, 1995), 'Guidelines relating to the reporting of recovered memories', *Bulletin of the Australian Psychological Society*, 20–21.

[6] McConkey, K. M. (1995), 'Hypnosis, memory and the ethics of uncertainty', *Australian Psychologist, 30*, 1, 1–10.

Appendix 2:

Professional Contacts

Below are listed some national and international contacts where enquiries can be directed in order to locate a reputable practitioner who is bound by professional ethics.

British Society of Experimental and Clinical Hypnosis

Dr Michael Heap
Royal Hallamshire Hospital
Sheffield South Yorkshire S10 2JF

British Society of Medical and Dental Hypnosis

Ms Rhona Jackson
17 Keppel View Road
Kimberworth
Rotherham

Scottish Branch

Dr Prem C. Misra
Parkhead Hospital
Salamansa Street
Glasgow G31 5ES

American Society of Clinical Hypnosis

Mr William Hoffman Jr.
Suite 291
2200 E Devon Ave
Des Plaines IL 60118-4534

American Society for Clinical and Experimental Hypnosis

Ms Eloise Bredder
6728 Old McLean Village Row
McLean VA 22101

Australian Society of Hypnosis

Dr Mark Earl
Austin Hospital
Heidelberg VIC 3084

Canadian Society of Hypnosis

Ms Glenda Labelle
7027 Edgemont Drive
Calgary
Alberta T3A 2H9

Irish Society for Clinical and Experimental Hypnosis

Dr M. O'Reagan
2 Ivyville
Douglas Road
Cork

Bibliography

Articles

American Medical Association, 'Report on memories of childhood abuse', *Contemporary Hypnosis* 43 (1995), 2, 114–17.

Andrews, B., Morton, J., Bekerian, D.A., Brewin, C.R., Davies, G.M. & Mollon, P., 'The recovery of memories in clinical practice: Experiences and beliefs of British Psychological Society practitioners', *The Psychologist* 8 (1995), 11, 507–8.

Australian Psychological Society. 'Guidelines relating to the reporting of recovered memories', Bulletin of the Australian Psychological Society (February 1995), 20–21.

Barber, T.X., 'Realities of stage hypnosis' in Zilbergeld, Edelstein & Aaroz, *Hypnosis*, Ch. 4.

Berecz, J., 'Hypnosis — Yes: SDAs should use it', *Spectrum* 23 (1994), 4, 40.

Bergin, A.E., 'Psychotherapy and religious values', *Journal of Consulting and Clinical Psychology* 48 (1993), 1, 95–105.

Bourbignon, E. & Evascus, T., 'Altered states of consciousness within a general evolutionary perspective: A holocultural analysis', *Behavioural Science Research* 12 (1977), 199–216.

Bower, S.G., Gilligan, G.E. & Monteiro, K.P., 'Selectivity of learning caused by affective states', *Journal of Experimental Psychology* 110 (1981), 45, 451–73.

Bowers, M.K., 'Friend of traitor? Hypnosis in the service of religion', *International Journal of Clinical and Experimental Hypnosis* 7 (1959), 205.

British Psychological Society, 'Stage hypnotism — no serious risk', *The Psychologist* 9 (1996), 1, 3.

Court, J.H., 'Discernment: Discerning between the emotional, the psychotic and the spiritual', *Renewal Journal* 7 (1996), 1, 53–62.

— 'Lord of the trance', *Journal of Psychology and Christianity* 10 (1991), 3, 261–5.

— 'A case of congregational healing', *Journal of Psychology and Christianity* 4 (1985), 2.

— 'Hypnosis and inner healing', *Journal of Christian Healing* 9 (1987), 2, 29–35.

— 'Hypnosis revisited', *Interchange* 34 (1984), 55–60.

Collison, D.R., 'A visit to Cos: In search of origins and traditions', *Australian Journal of Clinical and Experimental Hypnosis* 18 (1990), 2, 63–70.

Crawford, H.J., 'Cognitive and physiological flexibility: multiple pathways to hypnotic responsiveness' in Ghorkin, V., Netter, P., Eysenck, H. & Rosenthal, R. (eds), *Suggestion and suggestibility: theory and research* (New York, Springer 1989).

de Pascalis, V. & Marucci, F.S., '40-Hz EEG and focused attention: Implications for the study of hypnosis', XXV International Congress of Psychology (Brussels, 1992).

Dorman, J.W., 'Spiritual resources in hypnosis', presentation to the Tenth Annual Meeting of the American Society of Clinical Hypnosis (Des Plaines IL, 1967).

Epstein, S., 'Integration of the cognitive and the psychodynamic unconscious', *American Psychologist* 49 (1994), 8, 709–24.

Gibson, H., 'A recent British case of a man charged with rape and other sexual offences', *Contemporary Hypnosis* 9 (1992), 3, 139–48.

Graham, K.R., 'Perceptual processes and hypnosis: support for a cognitive-state theory based on laterality', in Edmonston, W.E. (ed), *Conceptual and investigative approaches to hypnosis and hypnotic phenomena. Annals of New York Academy of Sciences. 296 (1977), 274–83.*

Gruzelier, J. & Warren, K., 'Neuropsychological evidence of reductions on left frontal tests with hypnosis', *Psychological Medicine* 23 (1993), 93–101.

Heap, M., 'A case of death following stage hypnosis: analysis and implications', *Contemporary Hypnosis* 12 (1995), 2, 99–110.

— 'Four Victims', *British Journal of Experimental and Clinical Hypnosis* 2 (1984), 60–62.

— 'Another case of indecent assault by a lay hypnotherapist', *Contemporary Hypnosis* 12 (1992), 2, 92–8.

Henninger, P., 'Conditional handedness: Handedness changes in multiple personality disordered subject reflect shift in hemispheric dominance', *Consciousness and Cognition* (1992), 1, 265–87.

Hilgard, E.R., 'Hypnosis', *Annual Review of Psychology* 26 91975), 19–44.

Hogan, T., 'hypnosis and the celebration of the Eucharist: relationship and implications', Paper presented to the Annual Convention, Christian Association of Psychological Studies (CAPS-West 1992).

'Hypnotism' in *New Day International* (May 1988), p. 9.

Josselon, R., & Lieblich, A., 'Fettering the mind in the name of "science" ', *American Psychologist* 51 (1996), 6, 651–6.

Judd, F.K., Burrows, G.D. & Dennerstein, L., 'The dangers of hypnosis: A review', *Australian Journal of Clinical and Experimental Hypnosis* 13 (1985), 1, 1–5.

Kelly, A.A., 'Hypnosis and self-hypnosis' in Melton, J.G., Clark, J. & Kelly, A.A. (eds), *New Age Encyclopedia* (Detroit MI, Gale Research 1990).

Kirsch, I. & Lynn, S.J., 'The altered state of hypnosis', *American Psychologist* 50 (1995), 10, 846–85.

Krippner, S., 'Cross cultural perspectives on hypnotic-like procedures used by native healing practitioners' in Rhue, Lynn & Kirsch, *Handbook of clinical hypnosis.*

Larson, D.B. et al., 'Systematic analysis of research on religious variables in four major psychiatric journals, 1978–1982', *American Journal of Psychiatry* 143 (1986), 3, 329–34.

Leuner, H., 'Guided affective imagery', *American Journal of Psychotherapy* 23 (1969), 4–22.

Malony, H.N., 'A theology for hypnosis: A beginning enquiry', *Journal of Psychology and Christianity* 2 (1983), 1, 2–11.

— 'Inner healing' in Benner, *Baker encyclopedia of psychology*, p. 581.

Mangan, J.T., 'Hypnosis: A medico-moral evaluation', *Linacre Quarterly* 26 (1959), 39.

Mastrapa, S.C., 'Hypnosis — Maybe: if it's like prayer', *Spectrum* 23 (1994), 4, 49–50.

Matheson, G., 'Hypnosis' in Benner, *Baker encyclopedia of psychology*, p. 552.

— 'Hypnotic aspects of religious experiences', *Journal of Psychology and Theology* 7 (1979), 1, 13–21.

McConkey, K.M., 'Hypnosis, memory and the ethics of uncertainty', *Australian Psychologist* 30 (1995), 1, 1–10.

Mesmer, R., 'Hypnosis induced by a hypnotist', *Journal of Christian Healing* 9 (1987), 1, 51–3.

Morgan, C.M., 'Hypnotic susceptibility, EEG theta and alpha waves, and hemispheric specificity', in Burrows, G.D, Collison, D.R. & Dennerstein, L. (eds), *Hypnosis 1979: Proceedings of the 8th International Congress of Hypnosis and Psychosomatic Medicine* (Amsterdam, Elsevier/North Holland Biomedical Press).

—, Court, J.H. & Roberts, R., 'Cognitive restructuring: A technique for the relief of chronic tinnitus', *Australian Journal of Clinical and Experimental Hypnosis* 19 (1982), 1, 27–33.

Morgan, W.P., 'Hypnosis and sport psychology' in Rhue, Lynn & Kirsch, *Handbook of clinical hypnosis.*

Newbold, G., 'Hypnotherapy and Christian belief', *In the service of Medicine* 29 (1983) 2, 16–20.

Poltawska, W., 'Objectifying Psychotherapy', *Catholic Medical Quarterly* 42 (1992), 4, 18–23.

Provonsha, J., 'Hypnosis — No: It may be a sin', *Spectrum* 23 (1994), 4, 42–8.

Railo, W.S. & Unestahl, L.-E. V., 'The Scandinavian practice of sport psychology' in Klavora, M.P. (ed), *Coach, athlete and the sport psychologist* (Champaign IL, Human Kinetics 1979).

Scotford, R., 'Myths, memories and reality', *Contemporary Hypnosis* 12 (1995), 2, 137–42.

Shepperson, V.L., 'Paradox, parables, and change: One approach to Christian hypnotherapy', *Journal of Psychology and Theology* 9 (1981), 1, 3–11.

— 'Hypnotherapy' in Benner, *Baker encyclopedia of psychology.*

Tan, S.Y., 'Training in professional psychology: Diversity includes religion' in *Clinical Training in Professional Psychology*, National Council of Schools of Professional Psychology Conference Proceedings 91993), 183–96.

Toon, K., Fraise, J., McFetridge, M. & Alwin N., 'Memory or mirage? The FMS debate', *The Psychologist* 9 (1996), 2, 73–7.

Venn, J., 'Hypnosis for Christians', *Journal of Christian Healing* 8 (1986), 2, 3–6.

Walker, W.-L., 1'Hypnosis — the healer within', *Australian Journal of Clinical and Experimental Hypnosis* 21 (1993), 2, 15–21.

Watkins, J., 'The affect bridge: A hypnoanalytic technique', *International Journal of Clinical and Experimental Hypnosis* 19 (1971), 1, 21–7.

West, V., Fellows, B. & Eaton, S., 'The British Society of Experimental and Clinical Hypnosis: a national survey', *Contemporary Hypnosis* 12 (1995), 2, 137–42.

Winkelmann, M., 'A cross-cultural study of magico-religious practitioners' in Heinze, R.I. (ed), *Proceedings of the International Conference on Shamanism* (Berkeley CA, Independent Scholars of Asia 1984).

Worthington, E.V., Jr., Kurusu, T.A., McCullough, M.E. & Sandage, S.J., 'Empirical research on religion and psychotherapeutic processes and outcomes: A 10-year review and research prospectus', *Psychological Bulletin* 119 (1996), 3, 448–87.

Zinberg, N.E., 'The study of consciousness states: 'Problems and progress' in Zinberg, N.E. (ed), *Alternate states of consciousness* (New York, Free Press 1977).

Books

Aaroz, E.L., *Hypnosis and sex therapy* (New York, Brunner/Mazel 1982).

Alman, B.M., & Lambrou, P., *Self-hypnosis* (New York, Brunner/Mazel 1992).

Anderson, C.A., *Healing hypotheses* (New York, Garland Publishing 1993).

Bandler, R. & Grinder, J., *Frogs into princes* (Moab UT, Real People Press 1979).

Benner, D.G. (ed), *Baker encyclopedia of psychology* (Grand Rapids MI, Baker Book House 1985).

Bennett, D. & R., *The Holy Spirit and you* (Plainfield HJ, Logos International 1971).

Bobgan, M. & D., *Hypnosis and the Christian* (Minneapolis MN, Bethany House 1984).

— *The psychological way/The spiritual way* (Minneapolis MN, Bethany House 1972).

Brown P., *The hypnotic brain: hypnotherapy and social communication* (New Haven CT, Yale University Press 1991).

Collins, G., *The biblical basis of Christian counseling for people helpers* (Colorado Springs CO, NavPress 1993).

Diagnostic and statistical manual of mental disorders, 4th ed (Washington DC, American Psychiatric Press 1994).

Dixon, P., *Signs of revival* (Eastbourne, Kingsway 1994).
Dossey, L., *Prayer is good medicine: How to reap the benefits of healing prayer* (San Francisco, Harper 1996).
Edmonston, W.E., *The induction of hypnosis* (New York, Wiley 1986).
Ellenberger, H.F., *The discovery of the unconscious: The history and evolution of dynamic psychiatry* (New York, basic Books 1970).
Freeman, H.E., *Angels of light?* (Plainfield NJ, Logos International 1969).
Fuller, R.C., *Mesmerism and the American cure of souls* (University of Pennsylvania Press 1982).
Gross, R.D., (Psychology: the science of mind and behaviour (London, Hodder and Stoughton 1993).
Haley, J. (ed), *Advanced techniques of hypnosis and therapy* (New York, Grune and Stratton 1967).
Hammond, D.C., *Handbook of hypnotic suggestion and metaphors* (New York, W.W. Norton 1990).
Hart, A.D. & Hogan, T.F., *how to find help you need* (Grand Rapids MI, Zondervan 1995).
Hilgard, E.R., *Divided consciousness: Multiple controls in human thought and action* (New York, Wiley 1977).
Hull, C., *Hypnosis and suggestibility* (New York, Grove Press 1933).
Hunt, D. & McMahon, T.A., *The seduction of Christianity* (Eugene OR, Harvest House 1985).
Koch, K., *Christian counselling and occultism* (Michigan, Kregel 1972).
— *The devil's alphabet* (W. Germany, Evangelistic Publishers n.d.).
Korn, B.W., *Religion and hypnosis meet,* Panel presentation to the Seventh Annual Meeting of the American Society of Clinical Hypnosis (Philadelphia, Lippencott 1977).
Kroger, W.S., Clinical and experimental hypnosis (Philadelphia, Lippincott 1977).
Lankton, S., *The answer within: A clinical framework of Ericksonian hypnotherapy* (New York, Brunner/Mazel 1983).
Larson, R., *Acupuncture: The hypnotic and demonic* (Denver CO, Bob Larson 1975).
Laurence, J.R. & Perry, C., *Hypnosis, will and memory: a psycho-legal history* (New York, Guilford 1988).
Malony, H.N. & Lovekin, A.A., *Glossolalia: Behavioural science perspectives on speaking in tongues* (New York, Oxford University Press 1985).
McDowell, J. & Stewart, D., *Understanding the occult* (San Bernardino CA, Here's Life Publisher 1982).
Mikhaiel, N., *The Toronto Blessing: Slaying in the Spirit: The telling wonder* (Marrickville NSW, Southville Press 1995).
Morton, R.B., *Hypnosis and pastoral counseling* Los Angeles CA, Westwood Publishing 1980).
Murray, J.A.C., *An introduction to a Christian psychotherapy* (Edinburgh, T & T Clark).

North, C.S., Ryall, J.E.M., Ricci, D.A. & Wetzel, R.D. *Multiple personalities, multiple disorders* (New York, Oxford University Press 1993).

Otis, G.K., *Like a roaring lion* (Van Nuys, Time Light 1973).

Podmore, F., From Mesmer to Christian Science (New York, University Books 1909).

Reber, G., *The penguin dictionary of psychology* (Harmondsworth, Penguin 1985).

Reid, T.F., Vicker M., Laine, J.A. & Langstaff, A., *Seduction?? A biblical response* (New Wilmington PA, Son-Rise Publications 1986).

Religion and Hypnosis Meet, Panel discussion (1965), American Society of Clinical Hypnosis Proceedings (Des Plaines IL 1965), pp. 28–9.

Rhue, J.W., Lynn, S.J. & Kirsch, I. (eds), *Handbook of clinical hypnosis* (Washington DC, American Psychological Association 1993).

Roberts, A.O., *Messengers of God: The sensuous side of spirituality* (Newberg OR, Barclay Press 1996).

Rossi, E.L. (ed), *The collected papers of Milton H. Erickson, M.D.*. (New York, Irvington 1980).

Rubin, Z. & McNeil, E.B., *The psychology of being human* (New York, Harper and Row 1983).

Sanders, R.D. & Malony H.N., *Speak up: Christian assertiveness* (Philadelphia, Westminster Press 1985).

Sanders, S., *Clinical self-hypnosis: The power of words and images* (New York, Guildford Press 1991).

Sandford, J. & M., *A Comprehensive guide to deliverance and inner healing* (Grand Rapids MI, Chosen Books, 1992).

Scott, Peck, M., *People of the Lie* (New York, Simon and Schuster 1983).

Scroggs, J.R., *Key ideas in personality theory* (St Paul MN, West Publishing 1985).

Seamands, D.A., *Healing of memories* (Wheaton, IL, Victor Books 1985).

Schorr, J.E., Psychotherapy through imagery (New York, Theime-Stratton 1983).

Sheehan, P.W. & McConkey, K.M., *Hypnosis and experience: The exploration of phenomena and process* (Hillsdale NJ, Lawrence Erlbaum Associates 1982).

Singh, A., *Positive and negative effects in hypnosis: Some contributing variables*, Paper presented to the American Psychological Association Annual Convention (Los Angeles, August 1994).

Tan, S.Y. & Ortberg, J., *Understanding depression* (Grand Rapids MI, Baker Books 1995).

Thomas, K., *Religion and hypnosis meet*. Panel presentation to the Seventh Annual Meeting of the American Society of Clinical Hypnosis (Philadelphia 1964), p. 34.

Tweedie, D.F., *The Christian and the couch: An introduction to Christian logotherapy* (Grand Rapids MI, Baker Book House 1963).

Unestahl, L.-E., *New paths of sport learning and excellence* (Orebro, University Department of Sport and Psychology 1981).

Walter, H., *Hypnose: Theorien, neurophysiologische Korrelate und praktische Hinweise* (Stuttgart, Thieme 1992).

Weitzenhoffer, A.M., *The Practice of hypnotism*, 2 vols (New York, Wiley 1989).
Worthington, E.V., Jr., *Psychotherapy and religious values* (Grand Rapids MI, Baker Book House).
Wright, H.N., *Self-talk, imagery and prayer in counseling* (Dallas TX, Word 1986).
Yapko, M.D., *Essentials of hypnosis* (New York, Brunner/Mazel 1995).
Zilbergeld, B., Edelstein, M.G. & Aaroz, D.L. (eds), *Hypnosis: Questions and Answers* (New York, W.W. Norton 1986).
Zinberg, N.E., *Alternate states of consciousness* (New York, Free Press 1977).

Lightning Source UK Ltd.
Milton Keynes UK
UKOW07f1058090115

244189UK00011B/278/P